THE SECOND POST

BY THE SAME AUTHOR

ANTHOLOGIES

THE LADIES' PAGEANT
SOME FRIENDS OF MINE
THE GENTLEST ART

NOVELS

MR. INGLESIDE
OVER BEMERTON'S
LISTENER'S LURE

ESSAYS

ONE DAY AND ANOTHER
CHARACTER AND COMEDY

TRAVEL

A WANDERER IN PARIS
A WANDERER IN LONDON
A WANDERER IN HOLLAND
HIGHWAYS AND BYWAYS IN SUSSEX

STORIES FOR CHILDREN

ANNE'S TERRIBLE GOOD NATURE
THE SLOWCOACH

THE
SECOND
POST
"A COMPANION TO
THE GENTLEST ART"
E·V·LUCAS
"It's all very well to talk
of your Beethovens &
Mozarts. Very good in
their way, no doubt. But
for the music that counts
give me the double knock"
F.D. BEDFORD
NEW YORK: THE MACMILLAN COMPANY

Set up, electrotyped, and published October, 1910.

Norwood Press
J. S. Cushing Co. — Berwick & Smith Co.
Norwood, Mass., U.S.A.

PREFACE

THIS book is a supplement and companion to *The Gentlest Art*, an anthology of letters which was published in 1907. A list of persons to whom I am indebted for the use of copyright material appears at the end, but I should like here to thank them again, and also to draw attention to the new letters, now printed for the first time, which are to be found on pp. 224, 225, 229, 233, 234.

E. V. L.

CONTENTS

I. FROM AGE TO YOUTH

II. THE TRAVELLERS

III. ADONAIS GARRULOUS

Contents

IV. FIRST CENTURY A.D.

V. E. F.G.

VI. ELIA

VII. RURAL FELICITY

Contents

XV. THE OLD LION

XVI. LACONICS

XVII. WHIMSICALITIES

THE SECOND POST

I

FROM AGE TO YOUTH

The Rev. Sydney Smith sends a message to a little visitor

FOSTON, 1823

DEAR LITTLE GEE,—Many thanks for your kind and affectionate letter. I cannot recollect what you mean by our kindness; all that I remember is, that you came to see us, and we all thought you very pleasant, good-hearted, and strongly infected with Lancastrian tones and pronunciations. God bless you, dear child! I shall always be very fond of you till you grow tall, and speak without an accent, and marry some extremely disagreeable person.—Ever very affectionately yours,

SYDNEY SMITH

Landor and his son exchange missives

I

MY DEAREST PAPA,—I hope you are well. We have all had bad colds. But thank God we are now quite well again. Walter, Charles, and Julia send you a thousand kisses. And I send you ten thousand, and I wish you to come back again with all my heart. And believe me, my dearest papa, your affectionate son,

A. S. LANDOR

II

MY DEAREST ARNOLD,—I received your letter to-day much too late to answer it by the post; but you will see that I was thinking of you and of Julia yesterday by the verses I send you on the other side. I am very much pleased to observe that you write better than I do; and, if you continue to read the Greek nouns, you will very soon know more Greek [than I], unless I begin again to study it every day. When I was a little boy I did not let any one get before me; and you seem as if you would do the same. I promised you a Greek book, but I will give you two if you go on well, and next year two others, very beautiful and entertaining. I shall never be quite happy until I see you again and put my cheek upon your head. Tell my sweet Julia that, if I see twenty little girls, I will not romp with any of them before I romp with her; and kiss your two dear brothers for me. You must always love them as much as I love you, and you must teach them how to be good boys, which I cannot do so well as you can. God preserve and bless you, my own Arnold. My heart beats as if it would fly to you, my own fierce creature. We shall very soon meet.

Love your BABBO

The Rev. Sydney Smith offers counsel to Lucy

LONDON, *July* 22, 1835

LUCY, Lucy, my dear child, don't tear your frock: tearing frocks is not of itself a proof of genius; but write as your mother writes, act as your mother acts; be frank, loyal, affectionate, simple, honest; and then integrity or laceration of frock is of little import.

And Lucy, dear child, mind your arithmetic. You know, in the first sum of yours I ever saw, there was a mistake. You had carried two (as a cab is licensed to do) and you ought, dear Lucy, to have carried but one. Is this a trifle? What would life be without arithmetic, but a scene of horrors?

You are going to Boulogne, the city of debts, peopled by men who never understood arithmetic; by the time you return, I shall probably have received my first paralytic stroke, and shall have lost all recollection of you; therefore I now give you my parting advice. Don't marry anybody who has not a tolerable understanding and a thousand a year; and God bless you, dear child!

SYDNEY SMITH

Charles Dickens assures a young admirer of *Nicholas Nickleby* that all shall go well

(To Master Hastings Hughes)

DOUGHTY STREET, LONDON
December 12, 1838

RESPECTED SIR,—I have given Squeers one cut on the neck and two on the head, at which he appeared much surprised and began to cry, which, being a cowardly thing, is just what I should have expected from him — wouldn't you?

I have carefully done what you told me in your letter about the lamb and the two "sheeps" for the little boys. They have also had some good ale and porter, and some wine. I am sorry you didn't say *what* wine you would like them to have. I gave them some sherry which they liked very much, except one boy, who was a little sick and choked a good deal. He was rather greedy, and that's the truth, and I believe it went the wrong way, which I say served him right, and I hope you will say so too.

Nicholas had his roast lamb, as you said he was to, but he could not eat it all, and says if you do not mind his doing so he should like to have the rest hashed to-morrow with some greens, which he is very fond of, and so am I. He said he did not like to have his porter hot, for he thought it spoilt the flavour, so I let him have it cold. You should have seen him drink it. I thought he never would have left off. I also gave him three pounds of money, all in sixpences, to make it seem more, and he said directly that he should give more than half to his mamma and sister, and divide the rest with poor Smike. And I say he is a good fellow for saying so; and if anybody says he isn't I am ready to fight him whenever they like — there!

Fanny Squeers shall be attended to, depend upon it. Your drawing of her is very like, except that I don't think the hair is quite curly enough. The nose is particularly like hers, and so are the legs. She is a nasty disagreeable thing, and I know it will make her very cross when she sees it; and what I say is that I hope it may. You will say the same, I know — at least I think you will.

I meant to have written you a long letter, but I cannot write very fast when I like the person I am writing to, because that makes me think about them, and I like you, and so I tell you. Besides, it is just eight o'clock at night, and I always go to bed at eight o'clock except when it is my birthday, and then I sit up to supper. So

I will not say anything more beside this — and that is my love to you and Neptune; and if you will drink my health every Christmas Day I will drink yours — come. — I am, Respected Sir, your affectionate Friend,

CHARLES DICKENS

P.S. — I don't write my name very plain, but you know what it is, you know, so never mind.

Charles Dickens is forced to disappoint Miss Mary Talfourd

DEVONSHIRE TERRACE, *December* 16, 1841

MY DEAR MARY, — I should be delighted to come and dine with you on your birthday, and to be as merry as I wish you to be always; but as I am going, within a very few days afterwards, a very long distance from home, and I shall not see any of my children for six long months, I have made up my mind to pass all that week at home for their sakes; just as you would like your papa and mamma to spend all the time they possibly could spare with you if they were about to make a dreary voyage to America; which is what I am going to do myself.

But although I cannot come to see you on that day, you may be sure that I shall not forget that it is your birthday, and that I shall drink your health and many happy returns, in a glass of wine, filled as full as it will hold. And I shall dine at half-past five myself, so that we may both be drinking our wine at the same time; and I shall tell my Mary (for I have got a daughter of that name, but she is a very small one as yet) to drink your health too; and we shall try and make believe that you are here, or that we are in Russell Square, which is the best, thing we can do, I think, under the circumstances.

You are growing up so fast that by the time I come home again I expect you will be almost a woman; and in a very few years we shall be saying to each other: "Don't you remember what the birthdays used to be in Russell Square?" and "How strange it seems!" and "How quickly time passes!" and all that sort of thing, you know. But I shall always be very glad to be asked on your birthday, and to come if you will let me, and to send my love to you, and to wish that you may live to be very old and very happy, which I do now with all my heart. — Believe me always, my dear Mary, yours affectionately,
CHARLES DICKENS

Bishop Walsham How expresses his disappointment to the children of the Rev. Daniel Tyson

BUTTERED TOAST

THERE was a Bishop, old and grey,
Who came to Brighton one fine day,
And it chanced at the time there were living there
Three little maidens bright and fair,
And they were as merry as merry could be,
And the Bishop he loved them, one, two, three.
Now the Bishop he craftily planned to arrive
At the door of the house as the clock struck five,
For once on a time he had called at the door
At the very same hour two years before:
The master and mistress were out, you see,

And the children were having their nursery tea;
So he mounted, unbidden, the topmost stair,
And asked to partake of the children's fare;
And no words are potent enough to reveal
The exquisite bliss of that nursery meal!
The sweet little maidens were full of fun,
And the Bishop he loved them, three, two, one;
But that which enchanted his Lordship most
Was the hot, brown, well-buttered nursery toast!
Alas! for the words that now smote on his ear, —
"Not at home," not even the children dear!
So sadly he turned away from the door,
And he sighed to think that his dream was o'er;
And, as memories sweet of the past arose,
He brushed a tear from the end of his nose,
For he'd failed in his longing once more to see
Those sweet little maidens, one, two, three.
Yet the one soft vision that touched him most
Was the thought of that nursery buttered toast!

R. L. S. transfers his birthday rights

[The following letter was written to the American Land Commissioner (later Chief Justice for a term) in Samoa, whose younger daughter, then at home in the States, had been born on a Christmas Day, and consequently regarded herself as defrauded of her natural rights to a private anniversary of her own. — SIDNEY COLVIN.]

VAILIMA, *June* 19, 1891

DEAR MR. IDE, — Herewith please find the DOCUMENT, which I trust will prove sufficient in law. It seems to me very attractive in its eclecticism; Scots, English, and Roman law phrases are all indifferently introduced, and a quotation from the works of Haynes Bayly can hardly fail to attract the indulgence of the Bench. — Yours very truly,

ROBERT LOUIS STEVENSON

I, Robert Louis Stevenson, Advocate of the Scots Bar, author of *The Master of Ballantrae* and *Moral Emblems*, stuck civil engineer, sole owner and patentee of the Palace and Plantation known as Vailima in the island of Upolu, Samoa, a British subject, being in sound mind, and pretty well, I thank you, in body:

In consideration that Miss Annie H. Ide, daughter of H. C. Ide, the town of Saint Johnsbury, in the county of Caledonia, in the state of Vermont, United States of America, was born, out of all reason, upon Christmas Day, and is therefore out of all justice denied the consolation and profit of a proper birthday;

And considering that I, the said Robert Louis Stevenson, have attained an age when O, we never mention it, and that I have now no further use for a birthday of any description;

And in consideration that I have met H. C. Ide, the father of the said Annie H. Ide, and found him about as white a land commissioner as I require:

Have transferred, and *do hereby transfer*, to the said Annie H. Ide, *all and whole* my rights and privileges in the thirteenth day of November, formerly my birthday, now, hereby, and henceforth, the birthday of the said Annie H. Ide, to have, hold, exercise, and enjoy the same in the customary manner, by the sporting of fine raiment, eating of rich meats, and receipt of gifts, compliments, and copies of verse, according to the manner of our ancestors;

And I direct the said Annie H. Ide to add to the said name of Annie H. Ide the name Louisa — at least in private; and I charge her to use my said birthday with moderation and humanity, *et tamquam bona filia familiae*, the said birthday not being so young as it once was, and having carried me in a very satisfactory manner since I can remember;

And in case the said Annie H. Ide shall neglect or contravene either of the above conditions, I hereby revoke the donation and transfer my rights in the said birthday to the President of the United States of America for the time being;

In witness whereof I have hereto set my hand and seal this nineteenth day of June in the year of grace eighteen hundred and ninety-one.

ROBERT LOUIS STEVENSON

Witness, Lloyd Osbourne
Witness, Harold Watts

R. L. S. sets up a memory

NEW JERSEY, *May* 27, 1888

DEAR HOMER ST. GAUDENS, — Your father has brought you this day to see me, and he tells me it is his hope you may remember the occasion. I am going to do what I can to carry out his wish; and it may amuse you, years after, to see this little scrap of paper and to read what I write. I must begin by testifying that you yourself took no interest whatever in the introduction, and in the most proper spirit displayed a single-minded ambition to get back to play, and this I thought an excellent and admirable point in your character. You were also (I use the past tense, with a view to the time when you shall read, rather than to that when I am writing) a very pretty boy, and (to my European views) startlingly self-possessed. My time of observation was so limited that you must pardon me if I can say no more: what else I marked, what restlessness of foot and hand, what graceful clumsiness, what experimental designs upon the furniture, was but the common inheritance of human youth. But you may perhaps like to know that the lean flushed man in bed, who interested you so little, was in a state of mind extremely mingled and unpleasant: harassed with work which he thought he was not doing well, troubled with difficulties to which you will in time succeed, and yet looking forward to no less a matter than a voyage to the South Seas and the visitation of savage and desert islands. — Your father's friend,

ROBERT LOUIS STEVENSON

William Thomas, Clerk of the Council, tenders to Edward the Sixth a few questions the answers to which are useful to monarchs

TO THE KINGS HIGHNES, — Pleaseth your excellent Matie albeit that my grosse knowledge be utterly unapte to entreprise th' Instruction of any thinge unto your Highnes, whose erudicion I knowe to be suche as everie faithfull hert ought to rejoise at: yet imagining with myself that hitherto your Majestie hath more applied the studie of the tonges than any matter either of Historie or of Policie, (the Holie Scriptures excepted), and considering that (syns your Highnes is by the providence of God alreadie growen to the admynistracon of that great and famous chardge that hath been flete unto yow by your most noble Progenitors) there is no earthlie thinge more necessarie than the knowledge of such examples as in this and other regiments heretofore have happened: one thought of my bounden dutie I coulde no lesse do than present unto your Ma[tie] the Notes of those Discourses that nowe my principall studie, which I have gathered out of divers aucthors, entending with layssor to write the circumstances of those reasons that I can finde to make most for the purpose. And bicause there is nothing better learned than that which man laboureth for himself, therefore I determined at this present to give unto your Highnes this little Abstracte only. Trusting that liek as in all kinde of vertuouse Learning and Exercise ye have alwaies shewed yourself most diligent, even so in this parte which concerneth the chief mayntenance of your high astate, and preservacion of your Common Wealthe, your Majestie woll shewe no lesse industrie than the matter deserveth. For, though these be but Questions: yet there is not so small a one emongest them as woll not mynister matter of much discourse worthie the argument and debating; which your Highnes may either for passetyme or in earnest propone to the wisest men. And whan so ever there shall appeare any difficultie that your Majestie wolde have discussed, if it shall stande with your pleasour I shall most gladly write the circumstance of the best discourses that I can gather tooching that parte, and accordingly present it unto your Highnes: most humbly beseching the same to accepte my good will in as good parte as if I were of habilitie to offer unto yor Matie a more worthy thinge. — Yo^r^ Ma^ts^ most humble servaunt,

William Thomas

1. Whereof hath growen th' aucthoritie of Astates, and howe many kindes of Astates there be?

2. Which of all Astates is most commendable and necessarie?

3. Wheather a moltitude without heade may prosper?

4. Wheather is wiser and more constant, the Moltitude or the Prince?

5. Wheather is better for the Commonwealthe that the power be in the Nobilitie or in the people?

6. Wheather a meane Astate may beare a great subject?

7. What Lawes arr necessarie, and howe they ought to be mainteigned?

8. Howe easilie a weak Prince with good ordre may longe be mainteigned, and how esone a mightie Prince with little disordre may be destroied?

9. What causeth an inheritor King to loose his Realme?

10. Wheather Religion, besids the honor of God, be not also the gretest staie of Civile ordre? and wheather the Unitie thereof ought not to be preserved with the swearde and rigor?

11. Wheather of the twoo is the more unkinde, the People or the Prince?

12. Howe unkindenesse may be eschewed?

13. What is th' occasion of Conspiracies?

14. Wheather the People commonly desire the destruction of him that is in aucthoritie, and what moveth them so to do?

15. What a man of authoritie may do in the Moltitude?

16. What is to be observed in chooseng of Officers?

17. Howe flatterers arr to be knowen and despised?

18. Howe mennes opinions in great matters are to be pondered?

19. Wheather in Judgements the meane waie ought to be observed?

20. Wheather a man of aucthoritie ought to contempne his inferiors?

21. Howe dangerouse is it to leape from Humilitie unto Pride, and from Pride to Creweltie?

22. Wheather men may easelie be corrupted?

23. Howe much good mynisters ought to be rewarded and the evill punished?

24. Howe daungerouse it is be aucthor of a newe matter?

25. Wheather accusations arr necessarie, and wheather yll reaportes arr condempnable?

26. Wheather yll Reaporte lighteth not most commonly on the Reaporter?

27. Wheather ambitious men, mounting from one ambicion to an other, do first seeke not to be offended, and afterwards to offende?

28. Wheather it be daungerouse to make him an Officer that ones hath been misused?

29. Wheather they be not often deceaved that thinke with humilitie to overcome Pride?

30. What force the Prince's example hath emongest the Subjectes?

31. Howe a Prince ought to governe himself to attaigne reputacion?

32. What thinges deserve either praise or reproache?

33. What is Liberalitie and Miserie?

34. What is Creweltie and Clemencie?

35. Wheather Hate and Dispraise ought to be eschewed?

36. What is Fortune?

37. Howe men be oftentimes blinded with fortune?

38. Wheather it be not necessarie for him that woll have contynuall good fortune, to varie with the tyme?

39. What Prince's amytie is good?

40. Wheather a puissant Prince ought to purchase amitie with money? or with vertue and stowtenes?

41. What trust ought to be had in Leages?

42. What is the cause of Warre?

43. Howe many kindes of Warre there be?

44. Howe many kindes of Souldeors?

45. Wheather they that fight for their owne glorie arr good and faithfull souldeors?

46. Why do men overreune straunge countreys?

47. Howe shulde a Prince measure his force, and howe rule himself in warre?

48. Wheather a manifest warre towards, ought to be begoune upon th' ennemye, or abbiden till th' ennemye beginne?

49. Wheather is it better to assaulte or to defende?

50. Wheather money be the substaunce of warre or not?

51. Wheather weake Astates arr ever doubtfull in determyneng, and wheather much deliberacion doth rather hurte than helpe?

52. Wheather is greater in Conquest, vertue or fortune?

53. Wheather prevaileth more in fortune, Policie or Force?

54. What is Policie in warre?

55. Wheather Conquests arr not sometime more noysome than proffitable?

56. Wheather it be wisedome to adventure much?

57. What meanes ought to be used in defence?

58. Wheather the Countrey ought not alwaies to be defended, the quarell being right or wronge?

59. Wheather inconveniences ought rather to be qualified and overcome with layssour, or at the first plainely repressed?

60. What daungur is it to a Prince not to be avenged of an open Injurie?

61. What discommoditie is it to a Prince to lacke Armure?

62. Howe much ought Artillerie to be esteemed?

63. Wheather ought more to be esteemed, Footemen or Horsemen?

64. Wheather it be not daungerouse to be served of straunge souldeors?

65. Wheather is an Armie better governed of one absolute head, or of divers?

66. What ought the Generall of an Armie to be?

67. Wheather is more to be esteemed a good Captaine with a weake Armye, or a stronge Armye with a weak Captaine?

68. Wheather it be necessarie that generall Captaines have large commissions?

69. What advantage is it to foresee the ennemyes purpose?

70. Wheather a Captaine in the fielde may forsake the feight if his ennemye woll nedes feight?

71. What it is to be quick of Invention in the time of battaill?

72. What sufferaunce and tyme is in Feight.

73. Wheather it be necessarie to assure th' armie before the feight?

74. Wheather it be not necessarie sometime to feigne folie?

75. Howe to beware of crafte, when th' ennemie seemeth to have committed a folie?

76. What advauntage it is for a Captaine to knowe his grounde?

77. Wheather Skyrmisshes be good?

78. Wheather Fortresses arr not many times more noysome than proffitable?

79. Wheather an excellent man doth alter his cowraige for any adversitie?

80. Wheather Prince ought to be contented with resonable victories? and so to leave?

81. Wheather Furie and Braverie be many times necessarie to obteigne purposes?

82. Wheather promises made by force ought to be observed?

83. Wheather it becommeth not a Prince to pretende liberalitie when necessitie constreigneth him to depart with thinges.

84. What is vertue, and when is it most esteemed?

85. What destroieth the memorie of things?

It becometh a Prince for his wisdome to be had in admiracion as well of his chiefest Counsaillors as of his other subjects; and syns nothing serveth more to that than to kepe the principall things of wisedome secrett till occasion require the utterance, I wolde wishe them to be kept secret; referring it neverthelesse to your Majesties good will and pleasor.

II

THE TRAVELLERS

Shelley describes his life at Leghorn

LIVORNO, *August* (22?) 1819

MY DEAR PEACOCK, — I ought first to say that I have not yet received one of your letters from Naples; in Italy such things are difficult, but your present letter tells me all that I could desire to hear of your situation.

My employments are these: I awaken usually at seven; read half-an-hour; then get up; breakfast; after breakfast ascend *my tower*, and read or write until two. Then we dine. After dinner I read Dante with Mary, gossip a little, eat grapes and figs, sometimes walk, though seldom, and at half-past five pay a visit to Mrs. Gisborne, who reads Spanish with me until near seven. We then come for Mary, and stroll about till supper time. Mrs. Gisborne is a sufficiently amiable and very accomplished woman; she is *δημοκρατικη* and *αθεη* — how far she may be *φιλανθρωπη* I don't know, for she is the antipodes of enthusiasm. His (*sic*) husband, a man with little thin lips, receding forehead, and a prodigious nose, is an excessive bore. His nose is sometimes quite Slawkenbergian — it weighs on the imagination to look at it. It is that sort of nose which transforms all the g's its wearer utters into k's. It is a nose once seen never to be forgotten, and which requires the utmost stretch of Christian charity to forgive. I, you know, have a little turn-up nose; Hogg has a large hook one; but add them both together, square them, cube them, you would have but a faint idea of the nose to which I refer.

I most devoutly wish I were living near London. I do not think I shall settle so far off as Richmond; and to inhabit any intermediate spot on the Thames would be to expose myself to the river damps; not to mention that it is not much to my taste. My inclinations point to Hampstead; but I do not know whether I should not make up my mind to something more completely suburban. What are mountains, trees, heaths, or even the glorious and ever-beautiful sky, with such sunsets as I have seen at Hampstead, to friends? Social enjoyment, in some form or other, is the alpha and omega of existence. All that I see in Italy — and from my tower window I now see the magnificent peaks of the Apennines half enclosing the plain — is nothing; it dwindles into smoke in the mind, when I think of some familiar forms of scenery, little perhaps in themselves, over which old remembrances have thrown a delightful colour. How we prize what we despised when present! So the ghosts of our dead associations rise and haunt us, in revenge for our having let them starve, and abandoned them to perish.

You don't tell me if you see the Boinvilles; nor are they included in the list of the *conviti* at the monthly symposium. I will attend it in imagination.

One thing, I own, I am curious about; and in the

chance of the letters not coming from Naples, pray tell me. What is it you do at the India House? Hunt writes, and says you have got a *situation* in the India House: Hogg that you have an *honourable employment:* Godwin writes to Mary that you have got *so much or so much:* but nothing of what you do. The devil take these general terms. Not content with having driven all poetry out of the world, at length they make war on their own allies; nay, on their very parents, dry facts. If it had not been the age of generalities, any one of these people would have told me what you did.

I have been much better these last three weeks. My work on the "Cenci," which was done in two months, was a fine antidote to nervous medicines, and kept up, I think, the pain in my side, as sticks do a fire. Since then, I have materially improved. I do not walk enough. Clare, who is sometimes my companion, does not dress in exactly the right time. I have no stimulus to walk. Now, I go sometimes to Livorno on business; and that does me good.

I have been reading Calderon in Spanish. A kind of Shakespeare is this Calderon; and I have some thoughts if I find that I cannot do anything better, of translating some of his plays.

The *Examiners* I receive. Hunt, as a political writer, pleases me more and more. Adieu. Mary and Clare send their best remembrances. — Your most faithful friend,

P. B. SHELLEY

Pray send me some books, and Clare would take it as a great favour if you would send her *music books*.

Shelley numbers the inhabitants of Lord Byron's menagerie

RAVENNA, *August* 1821

MY DEAR PEACOCK, — I received your last letter just as I was setting off from the Bagni on a visit to Lord Byron at this place. Many thanks for all your kind attention to my accursed affairs. I am happy to tell you that my income is satisfactorily arranged, although Horace Smith having received it, and being still on his slow journey through France, I cannot send you, as I wished to have done, the amount of my debt immediately, but must defer it till I see him or till my September quarter, which is now very near. I am very much obliged to you for your way of talking about it — but of course, if I cannot do you any good, I will not permit you to be a sufferer by me.

I have sent by the Gisbornes a copy of the *Elegy on Keats*. The subject, I know, will not please you; but the composition of the poetry, and the taste in which it is written, I do not think bad. You and the enlightened public will judge. Lord Byron is in excellent cue both of health and spirits. He has got rid of all those melancholy and degrading habits which he indulged at Venice. He lives with one woman, a lady of rank here, to whom he is attached, and who is attached to him, and is in every respect an altered man. He has written three more cantos of "Don Juan." I have yet only heard the fifth, and I think that every word of it is pregnant with immortality. I have not seen his late plays, except "Marino Falieri," which is very well, but not so transcendently fine as the "Don Juan." Lord

Byron gets up at *two* I get up, quite contrary to my usual custom, but one must sleep or die, like Southey's sea-snake in "Kehama," at 12. After breakfast we sit talking till six. From six till eight we gallop through the pine forests which divide Ravenna from the sea; we then come home and dine, and sit up gossiping till six in the morning. I don't suppose this will kill me in a week or fortnight, but I shall not try it longer. Lord B.'s establishment consists, besides servants, of ten horses, eight enormous dogs, three monkeys, five cats, an eagle, a crow, and a falcon; and all these, except the horses, walk about the house, which every now and then resounds with their unarbitrated quarrels, as if they were the masters of it. Lord B. thinks you wrote a pamphlet signed "John Bull"; he says he knew it by the style resembling "Melincourt," of which he is a great admirer. I read it, and assured him that it could not possibly be yours. I write nothing, and probably shall write no more. It offends me to see my name classed among those who have no name. If I cannot be something better, I had rather be nothing, and the accursed cause, to the downfall of which I dedicate what powers I may have had, flourishes like a cedar and covers England with its boughs. My motive was never the infirm desire of fame; and if I should continue an author, I feel that I should desire it. This cup is justly given to one only of an age; indeed, participation would make it worthless: and unfortunate they who seek it and find it not.

I congratulate you — I hope I ought to do so — on your expected stranger. He is introduced into a rough world. My regards to Hogg, and Co[u]lson if you see him. — Ever most faithfully yours, P. B. S.

The Second Post

After I have sealed my letter, I find that my enumeration of the animals in this Circean Palace was defective, and that in a material point. I have just met on the grand staircase five peacocks, two guinea hens, and an Egyptian crane. I wonder who all these animals were before they were changed into these shapes.

Charles Dickens sends an American the news from America

FULLER'S HOTEL, WASHINGTON
Monday, March 14, 1842

MY DEAR FELTON, — I was more delighted than I can possibly tell you, to receive (last Saturday night) your welcome letter. We and the oysters missed you terribly in New York. You carried away with you more than half the delight and pleasure of my New World; and I heartily wish you could bring it back again.

There are very interesting men in this place — highly interesting, of course — but it's not a comfortable place; is it? If spittle could wait at table we should be nobly attended, but as that property has not been imparted to it in the present state of mechanical science, we are rather lonely and orphan-like, in respect of "being looked arter." A blithe black was introduced on our arrival, as our peculiar and especial attendant. He is the only gentleman in the town who has a peculiar delicacy in intruding upon my valuable time. It usually takes seven rings and a threatening message from —— to produce him; and when he comes, he goes to fetch something, and, forgetting it by the way, comes back no more.

We have been in great distress, really in distress, at the non-arrival of the *Caledonia.* You may conceive what our joy was, when, while we were out dining yesterday, Putnam arrived with the joyful intelligence of her safety. The very news of her having really arrived seemed to diminish the distance between ourselves and home, by one half at least.

And this morning (though we have not yet received our heap of despatches, for which we are looking eagerly forward to this night's mail) — this morning there reached us unexpectedly, through the Government bag (Heaven knows how they came there !), two of our many and long-looked-for letters, wherein was a circumstantial account of the whole conduct and behaviour of our pets; with marvellous relations of Charley's precocity at a Twelfth Night juvenile party at Macready's; and tremendous predictions of the governess, dimly suggesting his having got out of pot-hooks and hangers, and darkly insinuating the possibility of his writing us a letter before long; and many other workings of the same prophetic spirit, in reference to him and his sisters, very gladdening to their mother's heart, and not at all depressing to their father's. There was, also, the doctor's report, which was a clean bill; and the nurse's report, which was perfectly electrifying; showing as it did how Master Walter had been weaned, and had cut a double tooth, and done many other extraordinary things, quite worthy of his high descent. In short, we were made very happy and grateful; and felt as if the prodigal father and mother had got home again.

What do you think of this incendiary card being left at my door last night? "General G. sends compliments to Mr. Dickens, and called with two literary ladies. As the two L.L.'s are ambitious of the honour of a personal introduction to Mr. D., General G. requests the honour of an appointment for to-morrow." I draw a veil over my sufferings. They are sacred. We shall be in Buffalo, please Heaven, on the thirtieth of April. If I don't find a letter from you in the care of the postmaster at that place, I'll never write to you from England.

But if I *do* find one, my right hand shall forget its cunning before I forget to be your truthful and constant correspondent; not, dear Felton, because I promised it, nor because I have a natural tendency to correspond (which is far from being the case), nor because I am truly grateful to you for, and have been made truly proud by, that affectionate and elegant tribute which —— sent me, but because you are a man after my own heart, and I love you *well*. And for the love I bear you, and the pleasure with which I shall always think of you, and the glow I shall feel when I see your handwriting in my own home, I hereby enter into a solemn league and covenant to write as many letters to you as you write to me, at least. Amen.

Come to England! Come to England! Our oysters are small, I know; they are said by Americans to be coppery; but our hearts are of the largest size. We are thought to excel in shrimps, to be far from despicable in point of lobsters, and in periwinkles are considered to challenge the universe. Our oysters, small though they be, are not devoid of the refreshing influence which that species of fish is supposed to exercise in these latitudes. Try them and compare. — Affectionately yours,

CHARLES DICKENS

The Travellers

R. L. S. in San Francisco

January 10, 1880

MY DEAR COLVIN, — This is a circular letter to tell my estate fully. You have no right to it, being the worst of correspondents; but I wish to efface the impression of my last, so to you it goes.

Any time between eight and half-past nine in the morning, a slender gentleman in an ulster, with a volume buttoned into the breast of it, may be observed leaving No. 608 Bush and descending Powell with an active step. The gentleman is R. L. S.; the volume relates to Benjamin Franklin, on whom he meditates one of his charming essays. He descends Powell, crosses Market, and descends in Sixth on a branch of the original Pine Street Coffee House, no less; I believe he would be capable of going to the original itself, if he could only find it. In the branch he seats himself at a table covered with waxcloth, and a pampered menial, of High-Dutch extraction and, indeed, as yet only partially extracted, lays before him a cup of coffee, a roll and a pat of butter, all, to quote the deity, very good. A while ago, and R. L. S. used to find the supply of butter insufficient; but he has now learned the art to exactitude, and butter and roll expire at the same moment. For this refection he pays ten cents, or five pence sterling (£0, 0s. 5d.).

Half an hour later, the inhabitants of Bush Street observe the same slender gentleman armed, like George Washington, with his little hatchet, splitting, kindling, and breaking coal for his fire. He does this quasi-publicly upon the window-sill; but this is not to be attributed to any love of notoriety, though he is indeed vain of his prowess with the hatchet (which he persists in calling an axe), and daily surprised at the perpetuation of his fingers. The reason is this: that the sill is a strong, supporting beam, and that blows of the same emphasis in other parts of his room might knock the entire shanty into hell. Thenceforth, for from three to four hours, he is engaged darkly with an inkbottle. Yet he is not blacking his boots, for the only pair that he possesses are innocent of lustre and wear the natural hue of the material turned up with caked and venerable slush. The youngest child of his landlady remarks several times a day, as this strange occupant enters or quits the house, "Dere's de author." Can it be that this bright-haired innocent has found the true clue to the mystery? The being in question is, at least, poor enough to belong to that honourable craft.

His next appearance is at the restaurant of one Donadieu, in Bush Street, between Dupont and Kearney, where a copious meal, half a bottle of wine, coffee and brandy may be procured for the sum of four bits, *alias* fifty cents, £0, 2s. 2d. sterling. The wine is put down in a whole bottleful, and it is strange and painful to observe the greed with which the gentleman in question seeks to secure the last drop of his allotted half, and the scrupulousness with which he seeks to avoid taking the first drop of the other. This is partly explained by the fact that if he were to go over the mark — bang would go a ten-pence. He is again armed with a book, but his best friends will learn with pain that he seems at this hour to have deserted the more serious studies of the morning. When last observed, he was studying with apparent zest the exploits of one Rocambole by the late Viscomte Ponson du Terrail. This work, originally of prodigious dimensions, he had cut into liths or thicknesses apparently for convenience of carriage.

Then the being walks, where is not certain. But by half-past four, a light beams from the windows of 608 Bush, and he may be observed sometimes engaged in correspondence, sometimes once again plunged in the mysterious rites of the forenoon. About six he returns to the Branch Original, where he once more imbrues himself to the worth of fivepence in coffee and roll. The evening is devoted to writing and reading, and by eleven or half-past darkness closes over this weird and truculent existence.

As for coin, you see I don't spend much, only you and Henley both seem to think my work rather bosh nowadays, and I do want to make as much as I was making, that is £200; if I can do that, I can swim: last year, with my ill health I touched only £109; that would not do, I could not fight it through on that; but on £200, as I say, I am good for the world, and can even in this quiet way save a little, and that I must do. The worst is my health; it is suspected I had an ague chill yesterday; I shall know by to-morrow, and you know if I am to be laid down with ague the game is pretty well lost. But I don't know; I managed to write a good deal down in Monterey, when I was pretty sickly most of the time, and by God, I'll try, ague and all. I have to ask you frankly, when you write, to give me any good news you can, and, chat a little, but *just in the meantime*, give me no bad. If I could get *Thoreau*, *Emigrant* and *Vendetta* all finished and out of my hand, I should feel like a man who had made half a year's income in a half year; but until the last two are *finished*, you see, they don't fairly count.

I am afraid I bore you sadly with this perpetual talk about my affairs; I will try and stow it; but you see, it touches me nearly. I'm the miser in earnest now: last night, when I felt so ill, the supposed ague chill, it seemed strange not to be able to afford a drink. I would have walked half a mile, tired as I felt, for a brandy and soda. — Ever yours,
R. L. S.

R. L. S. fixes his ambition

(To R. A. M. Stevenson)

SARANAC LAKE, ADIRONDACKS
October 1887

MY DEAR BOB, — The cold [of Colorado] was too rigorous for me; I could not risk the long railway voyage, and the season was too late to risk the Eastern, Cape Hatteras side of the steamer one; so here we stuck and stick. We have a wooden house on a hill-top, overlooking a river, and a village about a quarter of a mile away, and very wooded hills; the whole scene is very Highland, bar want of heather and the wooden houses.

I have got one good thing of my sea voyage: it is proved the sea agrees heartily with me, and my mother likes it; so if I get any better, or no worse, my mother will likely hire a yacht for a month or so in summer. Good Lord! What fun! Wealth is only useful for two things: a yacht and a string quartette. For these two I will sell my soul. Except for these I hold that £700 a year is as much as anybody can possibly want; and I have had more, so I know, for the extry coins were of no use, excepting for illness, which damns everything.

The Travellers

I was so happy on board that ship, I could not have believed it possible. We had the beastliest weather, and many discomforts; but the mere fact of its being a tramp-ship gave us many comforts; we could cut about with the men and officers, stay in the wheel-house, discuss all manner of things, and really be a little at sea. And truly there is nothing else. I had literally forgotten what happiness was, and the full mind — full of external and physical things, not full of cares and labours and rot about a fellow's behaviour. My heart literally sang; I truly care for nothing so much as for that. We took so north a course, that we saw Newfoundland; no one in the ship had ever seen it before.

It was beyond belief to me how she rolled; in seemingly smooth water, the bell striking, the fittings bounding out of our state room. It is worth having lived these last years, partly because I have written some better books, which is always pleasant, but chiefly to have had the joy of this voyage. I have been made a lot of here, and it is sometimes pleasant, sometimes the reverse; but I could give it all up, and agree that —— was the author of my works, for a good seventy ton schooner and the coins to keep her on. And to think there are parties with yachts who would make the exchange! I know a little about fame now; it is no good compared to a yacht; and anyway there is more fame in a yacht, more genuine fame; to cross the Atlantic and come to anchor in Newport (say) with the Union Jack, and go ashore for your letters and hang about the pier, among the holiday yachtsmen — that's fame, that's glory, and nobody can take it away; they can't say your book is bad; you *have* crossed the Atlantic. I should do it south by the West Indies, to avoid the damned Banks; and probab'y come home by steamer, and leave the skipper to bring the yacht home.

Well, if all goes well, we shall maybe sail out of Southampton water some of these days and take a run to Havre, and try the Baltic or somewhere.

Love to all. — Ever your afft.

ROBERT LOUIS STEVENSON

III

ADONAIS GARRULOUS

I

(To John Hamilton Reynolds)

CARISBROOKE, *April* 17, 1817

MY DEAR REYNOLDS, — Ever since I wrote to my brothers from Southampton, I have been in a taking, and at this moment I am about to become settled, for I have unpacked my books, put them into a snug corner, pinned up Haydon, Mary Queen of Scots, and Milton with his daughters in a row. In the passage I found a head of Shakspeare, which I had not before seen. It is most likely the same that George spoke so well of, for I like it extremely. Well — this head I have hung over my books, just above the three in a row, having first discarded a French Ambassador: now this alone is a good morning's work. Yesterday I went to Shanklin, which occasioned a great debate in my mind whether I should live there or at Carisbrooke. Shanklin is a most beautiful place; sloping wood and meadow ground reach round the Chine, which is a cleft between the Cliffs of the depth of nearly 300 feet at least. This cleft is filled with trees and bushes in the narrow part, and as it widens becomes bare, if it were not for primroses on one side, which spread to the very verge of the Sea, and some fishermen's huts on the other, perched midway in the Balustrades of beautiful green Hedges along their steps down to the sands. But the sea, Jack, the sea — the little waterfall — then the white cliff — then St. Catherine's Hill — "the sheep in the meadows, the cows in the corn."

Then, why are you at Carisbrooke? say you. Because, in the first place, I should be at twice the Expense, and three times the inconvenience — next that from here I can see your continent from a little hill close by, the whole north Angle of the Isle of Wight, with the water between us. In the third place, I see Carisbrooke Castle from my window, and have found several delightful wood-alleys, and copses, and quick freshes. As for primroses, the Island ought to be called Primrose Island — that is, if the nation of Cowslips agree thereto, of which there are divers Clans just beginning to lift up their heads. Another reason of my fixing is, that I am more in reach of the places around me. I intend to walk over the Island East — West — North — South. I have not seen many specimens of Ruins — I don't think however I shall ever see one to surpass Carisbrooke Castle. The trench is overgrown with the smoothest turf and the Walls with ivy. The keep within side is one Bower of ivy — a colony of Jacdaws have been there for many years. I dare say I have seen many a descendant of some old cawer who peeped through the bars at Charles the First, when he was there in Confinement. On the road from Cowes to Newport I saw some extensive Barracks, which disgusted me extremely with the Government for placing such a Nest of Debauchery in so beautiful a place. I asked a man on the coach about this — and he said that the people had been spoiled. In the room where I slept at Newport, I found this on the window — "O Isle spoilt by the Mil*a*tary!" I must in honesty however confess that I did not feel very sorry at the idea of the women being a little profligate.

The wind is in a sulky fit, and I feel that it would be no bad thing to be the favourite of some Fairy, who would give one the power of seeing how our Friends got on at a distance. I should like, of all Loves, a sketch of you and Tom and George in ink which Haydon will do if you will tell him how I want them. From want of regular rest I have been rather *narvus* — and the passage in *Lear* — "Do you not hear the sea?" has haunted me intensely.

It keeps eternal whispering around
Desolate shores, and with its mighty swell
Gluts twice ten thousand Caverns, till the spell
Of Hecate leaves them their old shadowy sound.
Often 'tis in such gentle temper found,
That scarcely will the very smallest shell
Be mov'd for days from whence it sometime fell,
When last the winds from Heaven were unbound.
O ye! who have your eye-balls vex'd and tir'd,
Feast them upon the wideness of the Sea;
O ye! whose ears are dinn'd with uproar rude,
Or fed too much with cloying melody —
Sit ye near some old Cavern's Mouth, and brood
Until ye start, as if the sea-nymphs quired.

II

April 18 (1817)

WILL you have the goodness to do this? Borrow a Botanical Dictionary — turn to the words Laure and Prunus, shew the explanations to your sisters and

Mrs. Dilke and without more ado let them send me the Cups, Basket and Books they trifled and put off and off while I was in Town. Ask them what they can say for themselves — ask Mrs. Dilke wherefore she does so distress me — let me know how Jane has her health — the weather is unfavourable for her, — tell George and Tom to write. I'll tell you what — on the 23rd was Shakespeare born. Now if I should receive a letter from you, and another from my Brothers on that day 'twould be a parlous good thing. Whenever you write say a word or two on some Passage in Shakespeare that may have come rather new to you, which must be continually happening, notwithstanding that we read the same play forty times — for instance, the following from the Tempest never struck me so forcibly as at present:

> "Urchins
> *Shall, for the vast of night that they may work,*
> All exercise on thee ——"

How can I help bringing to your mind the line —

> "*In the dark backward and abysm of time.*"

I find I cannot exist without Poetry — without eternal Poetry — half the day will not do — the whole of it — I began with a little but habit has made me a Leviathan. I had become all in a tremble from not having written any thing of late. The Sonnet over-leaf did me good. I slept the better last night for it — this morning, however, I am nearly as bad again. Just now I opened Spenser, and the first lines I saw were these —

> "The noble heart that harbours virtuous thought,
> And is with child of glorious great intent,
> Can never rest until it forth have brought
> Th' eternal brood of glory excellent ——"

Let me know particularly about Haydon, ask him to write to me about Hunt, if it be only ten lines — I hope all is well — I shall forthwith begin my Endymion, which I hope I shall have got some way with by the time you come, when we will read our verses in a delightful place I have set my heart upon, near the Castle.

Give my Love to your Sisters severally — to George and Tom. Remember me to Rice, Mr. and Mrs. Dilke and all we know. — Your sincere friend,

John Keats

III

(To John Hamilton Reynolds)

Teignmouth, *Saturday* (*March* 14, 1818)

DEAR REYNOLDS, — I escaped being blown over and blown under and trees and house being toppled on me. — I have, since hearing of Brown's accident had an aversion to a dose of parapet, and being also a lover of antiquities I would sooner have a harmless piece of Herculaneum sent me quietly as a present than ever so modern a chimney-pot tumbled on to my head. Being agog to see some Devonshire, I would have taken a walk the first day, but the rain would not let me; and the second, but the rain would not let me; and the third, but the rain forbade it. Ditto 4 — ditto 5 — ditto — so I made up my Mind to stop in-doors, and catch a sight flying between the showers: and, behold I saw a pretty valley — pretty cliffs, pretty Brooks, pretty Meadows, pretty trees, both standing as they were created, and blown down as they are uncreated. The green is beautiful as they say, and pity it is that it is amphibious — *mais!* but alas! the flowers here wait as naturally for the rain twice a day as the Mussels do for the Tide; so we look upon a brook in these parts as you look upon a splash in your Country. There must be something to support this — aye, fog, hail, snow, rain, Mist blanketing up three parts of the year. This Devonshire is like Lydia Languish, very entertaining when it smiles but cursedly subject to sympathetic moisture. You have the sensation of walking under one great Lamp-lighter; and you can't go on the other side of the ladder to keep your frock clean, and cosset your superstition. Buy a girdle — put a pebble in your mouth — loosen your braces — for I am going among scenery whence I intend to tip you the Damosel Radcliffe — I'll cavern you, and grotto you, and waterfall you, and wood you, and water you, and immense-rock you, and tremendous-sound you, and solitude you. I'll make a lodgment on your glacis by a row of Pines, and storm your covered way with bramble Bushes. I'll have at you with hip and haw small-shot, and cannonade you with Shingles — I'll be witty upon salt-fish, and impede your cavalry with clotted cream. But ah coward! to talk at this rate to a sick man, or, I hope to one that was sick — for I hope by this you stand on your right foot. If you are not — that's all — I intend to cut all sick people if they do not make up their minds to cut Sickness — a fellow to whom I have a complete aversion, and who strange to say is harboured and countenanced in several houses where I visit — he is sitting now quite impudent between me and Tom — he insults me at poor Jem Rice's — and you have seated him before now between us at the Theatre, when I thought he looked with a longing eye at poor Kean. I shall say, once for all, to my friends, generally and severally, cut that fellow, or I cut you.

I went to the Theatre here the other night, which I

forgot to tell George, and got insulted, which I ought to remember to forget to tell any Body; for I did not fight, and as yet have had no redress — " Lie thou there, sweet-heart!" I wrote to Bailey yesterday, obliged to speak in a high way, and a damme who's afraid — for I had owed him so long; however, he shall see I will be better in future. Is he in town yet? I have directed to Oxford as the better chance. I have copied my Fourth Book, and shall write the Preface soon. I wish it was all done; for I want to forget it, and make my mind free for something new.

Atkins the coachman, Bartlett the surgeon, Simmons the barber, and the Girls over at the Bonnet shop, say we shall now have a month of seasonable weather — warm, witty and full of invention. Write to me and tell me that you are well or thereabouts, or by the holy Beaucœur, which I suppose is the Virgin Mary, or the repented Magdalen (beautiful name, that Magdalen), I'll take to my wings and fly away to anywhere but old or Nova Scotia. I wish I had a little innocent bit of metaphysic in my head, to criss-cross this letter, but you know a favourite tune is hardest to be remembered when one wants it most and you, I know, have long ere this taken it for granted that I never have any speculations without associating you in them, where they are of a pleasant nature, and you know enough of me to tell the places where I haunt most, so that if you think for five minutes after having read this, you will find it a long letter, and see written in the Air before you, your most affectionate friend,

JOHN KEATS

IV

(To the Misses M. and S. Jeffrey)

TEIGNMOUTH, HAMPSTEAD, *June* 4 (1818)

MY DEAR GIRLS, — I will not pretend to string a list of excuses together for not having written before — but must at once confess the indolence of my disposition, which makes a letter more formidable to me than a Pilgrimage. I am a fool in delay, for the idea of neglect is an everlasting Knapsack which even now I have scarce power to hoist off. By the bye, talking of everlasting knapsacks, I intend to make my fortune by them in a case of a War (which you must consequently pray for) by contracting with Government for said materials to the economy of one branch of the Revenue. At all events a Tax which is taken from the people and shoulder'd upon the military ought not to be snubb'd at I promised to send you all the news. Harkee! The whole city corporation, with a deputation from the Fire Offices, are now engaged at the London Coffee house in secret conclave concerning Saint Paul's Cathedral its being washed clean. Many interesting speeches have been demosthenized in said Coffee house as to the cause of the black appearance of the said Cathedral. One of the veal-thigh Aldermen actually brought up three witnesses to depose how they beheld the ci-devant fair Marble turn black on the tolling of the great Bell for the amiable and tea-table lamented Princess — adding moreover that this sort of sympathy in inanimate objects was by no means uncommon, for, said the Gentleman, "as we were once debating in the Common Hall Mr. Waitheman in illustration of some case in point quoted Peter Pindar, at which the head of George the third although in hard marble squinted over the Mayor's seat at the honourable speaker so oddly that he was obliged to sit down." However I will not tire you about these Affairs for they must be in your Newspapers by this time. You see how badly I have written these last three lines so I will remain here and take a pinch of snuff every five Minutes until my head becomes fit and proper and legitimately inclined to scribble. Oh! there's nothing like a pinch of snuff except perhaps a few trifles almost beneath a philosopher's dignity such as a ripe Peach or a Kiss that one takes on a lease of 91 moments — on a building lease. Talking of that, is the Cap^{n} married yet, or rather married? Miss Mitchell — is she stony hearted enough to hold out this season? Has the Doctor given Miss Perryman a little love powder? tell him to do so. It really would not be unamusing to see her languish a little — Oh she must be quite melting this hot Weather. Are the little Robins weaned yet? Do they walk alone? You have had a christening a top o' the tiles and a Hawk has stood God father and taken the little Brood under the Shadow of its Wings much in the way of Mother Church — a Cat too has very tender bowels in such pathetic Cases. They say we are all (that is our set) mad at Hampstead. There's George took unto himself a wife a week ago and will in a little time sail for America — and I with a friend am preparing for a four months' walk all over the North — and belike Tom not stop here — he has been getting much better — Lord what a Journey I had and what a relief at the end of it — I'm sure I could not have stood it many more days. Hampstead is now in fine order.

I suppose Teignmouth and the *contagious* country is

now quite remarkable — you might praise it I dare say in the manner of a grammatical exercise — *The* trees *are* full — *the* den *is* crowded — *the* boats *are* sailing — *the* musick *is* playing. I wish you were here a little while — but lauk we haven't got any female friend in the house. Tom is taken for a Madman and I being somewhat stunted am taken for nothing — We lounge on the Walk opposite as you might on the Den — I hope the fine season will keep up your mother's Spirits — she was used to be too much downhearted. No Women ought to be born into the world for they may not touch the bottle for shame — now a man may creep into a bung hole — However this is a tale of a tub — however I like to play upon a pipe sitting upon a puncheon and intend to be so drawn in the frontispiece to my next book of Pastorals — My Brother's respects and mine to your Mother and all our Loves to you. — Yours very sincerely,

JOHN KEATS

P.S. has many significations — here it signifies Post Script — in the corner of a Handkerchief Polly Saunders — upon a Garter Pretty Secret — upon a Band Box Pink Sattin — at the Theatre Princes Side — on a Pulpit Parson's Snuffle — and at a Country Ale House Pail Sider.

V

(To Thomas Keats)

AUCHENCAIRN, *July* 3 (1818)

MY DEAR TOM, — We are now in Meg Merrilies' country, and have, this morning, passed through some parts exactly suited to her. Kirkcudbright County is very beautiful, very wild, with craggy hills, somewhat in the Westmoreland fashion. We have come down from Dumfries to the sea-coast part of it. . . .

Yesterday was passed in Kirkcudbright; the country is very rich, very fine and with a little of Devon. I am now writing at Newton Stewart, six miles into Wigtown. Our landlady of yesterday said, "Very few Southerners passed hereaways." The children jabber away, as if in a foreign language; the barefooted girls look very much in keeping, — I mean with the scenery about them. Brown praises their cleanliness and appearance of comfort, the neatness of their cottages, etc. — it may be — they are very squat among trees and fern and heath and broom, on level slopes and heights — but I wish they were as snug as those up the Devonshire valleys. We are lodged and entertained in great varieties. We dined yesterday on dirty bacon, dirtier eggs, and dirtiest potatoes, with a slice of salmon — we breakfast this morning in a nice carpeted room, with sofa, hair-bottomed Chairs, and green-baized Mahogany. A spring by the road-side is always welcome. We drink water for dinner, diluted with a Gill of whisky.

July 6 (1818). — Yesterday morning we set out from Glenluce, going some distance round to see some rivers: they were scarcely worth the while. We went on to Stranraer, in a burning sun, and had gone about six miles when the Mail overtook us. We got up, were at Port Patrick in a jiffey, and I am writing now in little Ireland. The dialects on the neighbouring shores of Scotland and Ireland are much the same, yet I can perceive a great difference in the nations, from the chambermaid at this *nate toone* kept by Mr. Kelly. She is fair, kind and ready to laugh, because she is out of the horrible dominion of the Scotch Kirk. A Scotch girl stands in terrible awe of the Elders — poor little Susannahs, they will scarcely laugh, their Kirk is greatly to be damned. These Kirkmen have done Scotland good (query ?). They have made men, women; old men, young men; old women, young women; boys, girls; and all infants careful — so that they are formed into regular phalanges of savers and gainers. Such a thrifty army cannot fail to enrich their Country, and give it a greater appearance of comfort than that of their [this ?] poor rash neighbourhood. These Kirkmen have done Scotland harm; they have banished puns, and laughing, and kissing, etc. (except in cases where the very danger and crime must make it very gustful). I shall make a full stop at kissing, for after that, there should be a better parenthesis, and go on to remind you of the fate of Burns — poor unfortunate fellow, his disposition was Southern — how sad it is when a luxurious imagination is obliged, in self-defence, to deaden its delicacy in vulgarity and in things attainable, that it may not have leisure to go mad after things that are not. No man, in such matters, will be content with the experience of others. It is true that out of suffering there is no dignity, no greatness, that in the most abstracted pleasure there is no lasting happiness. Yet who would not like to discover over again that Cleopatra was a Gipsy, Helen a rogue, and Ruth a deep one? I have not sufficient reasoning faculty to settle the doctrine of thrift, as it is consistent with the dignity of human Society — with the happiness of Cottagers. All I can do is by plump contrasts; were the fingers made to squeeze a guinea or a white hand? — were the lips made to hold a pen or a kiss? and yet in Cities man is shut out from his fellows if he is poor — the cottages must be very dirty and very wretched if she be not thrifty — the present state of society demands this, and this convinces me the world is very young, and in a very ignorant state. We live in a barbarous age — I would sooner be a wild deer, than a girl under the dominion of the Kirk; and I would sooner be a wild hog, than be the occasion of a poor Creature's penance before those execrable elders.

VI

(To Fanny Keats)

WINCHESTER, *August* 28
Postmark, *August* 29, 1819

MY DEAR FANNY, — You must forgive me for suffering so long a space to elapse between the dates of my letters. It is more than a fortnight since I left Shanklin chiefly for the purpose of being near a tolerable Library, which after all is not to be found in this place. However we like it very much: it is the pleasantest Town I ever was in, and has the most recommendations of any. There is a fine Cathedral which to me is always a source of amusement, part of it built 1400 years ago; and the more modern by a magnificent Man, you may have read of in our History, called William of Wickham. The whole town is beautifully wooded. From the hill at the eastern extremity you see a prospect of Streets, and old Buildings mixed up with Trees. Then there are the most beautiful streams about I ever saw — full of Trout. There is the Foundation of St. Croix about half a mile in the fields — a charity greatly abused.

We have a Collegiate School, a Roman Catholic

School; a chapel ditto and a nunnery! And what improves it all is, the fashionable inhabitants are all gone to Southampton. We are quiet — except a fiddle that now and then goes like Gimlet through my Ears — our Landlady's son not being quite a Proficient.

The delightful Weather we have had for two Months is the highest gratification I could receive — no chill'd red noses — no shivering — but fair atmosphere to think in — a clean towel mark'd with the mangle and a basin of clear Water to drench one's face with ten times a day: no need of much exercise — a Mile a day being quite sufficient. My greatest regret is that I have not been well enough to bathe though I have been two Months by the sea side and live now close to delicious bathing. Still I enjoy the Weather — I adore fine Weather as the greatest blessing I can have. Give me Books, fruit, French wine and fine weather and a little music out of doors played by some one I do not know — not pay the price of one's time for a jig — but a little chance music: and I can pass a summer very quietly without caring much about Fat Louis, fat Regent or the Duke of Wellington.

Why have you not written to me? Because you were in expectation of George's letter and so waited? Mr. Brown is copying out our Tragedy of Otho the Great in a superb style — better than it deserves — there as I said is labour in vain for the present. I had hoped to give Kean another opportunity to shine. What can we do now? There is not another actor of Tragedy in all London or Europe. The Covent Garden Company is execrable. Young is the best among them and he is a ranting coxcombical tasteless Actor — a Disgust, a Nausea — and yet the very best after Kean. What a set of barren asses are actors! I should like now to promenade round your Gardens — apple-tasting — pear-tasting — plum-judging — apricot-nibbling — peach-scrunching — nectarine-sucking and melon-carving. I have also a great feeling for antiquated cherries full of sugar cracks — and a white currant tree kept for company. I admire lolling on a lawn by a water-lilied pond to eat white currants and see gold fish: and go to the Fair in the Evening if I'm good. There is not hope for that — one is sure to get into some mess before evening. Have these hot days I brag of so much been well or ill for your health? Let me hear soon. — Your affectionate Brother, JOHN

IV

FIRST CENTURY A.D.

Four Letters of Pliny the Younger

(To Bebius)

MY friend and guest Tranquillus has an inclination to purchase a small farm, of which, as I am informed, an acquaintance of yours intends to dispose.

I beg you would endeavour he may obtain it on reasonable terms; which will add to his satisfaction in the purchase. A dear bargain is always disagreeable, particularly as it is a reflection on the buyer's judgment.

There are several circumstances attending this little villa, which (supposing my friend has no objection to the price) are extremely suitable to his tastes and desires; the convenient distance from Rome, the goodness of the roads, the smallness of the building, and the very few acres of land around it, which are enough to amuse, but not to employ him.

To a man of the literary turn that Tranquillus is it is sufficient if he has but a small spot to relieve the mind and divert the eye, where he may saunter round his grounds, traverse his single walk, grow familiar with his two or three vines, and count his little plantations. I mention these particulars to let you see how much he will be obliged to me, as I shall be to you, if you can help him to this convenient little box, at a price of which he shall have no occasion to repent. Farewell.

(To Priscus)

As I know you gladly embrace every opportunity of obliging me, so there is no man to whom I had rather lay myself under an obligation.

I apply to you, therefore, preferably to anybody else, for a favour which I am extremely desirous of obtaining. You, who are at the head of a very considerable army, have many opportunities of exercising your generosity; and the length of time you have enjoyed that post, must have enabled you to provide for all your own friends. I hope you will now turn your eyes upon some of mine: they are but a few indeed for whom I shall solicit you; though your generous disposition, I know, would be better pleased if the number were greater. But it would ill become me to trouble you with recommending more than one or two; at present I will only mention Voconius Romanus. His father was of great distinction among the Roman knights; and his father-in-law, or, as I might more properly call him, his second father (for his affectionate treatment of Voconius entitles him to that appellation), was still more conspicuous. His mother was one of the most considerable ladies of Upper Spain: you know what character the people of that province bear, and how remarkable they are for the strictness of their manners. As for himself, he has been lately admitted into the sacred order of priesthood. Our friendship began with our studies, and we were early united in the closest intimacy. We lived together under the same roof in town and country, as he shared with me my most serious and my gayest hours: and where, indeed, could I have found a more faithful friend, or more agreeable companion? In his conversation, even in his very voice and countenance, there is the most amiable sweetness; as at the bar he discovers an elevated genius, an easy and harmonious elocution, a clear and penetrating apprehension. He has so happy a turn for epistolary writing, that were you to read his letters, you would imagine they had been dictated by the Muses themselves. I love him with more than common affection, and I know he returns it with equal ardour. Even in the earlier part of our lives, I warmly embraced every opportunity of doing him all the good offices which then lay in my power; as I have lately obtained for him of the Emperor, the privilege granted to those who have three children. A favour which though Cæsar very rarely bestows, and always with great caution, yet he conferred at my request, in such a manner as to give it the air and grace of being his own choice. The best way of shewing that I think he deserves the obligations he has already received from me, is by adding more to them, especially as he always accepts my favours with so much gratitude as to merit farther. Thus I have given you a faithful account of Romanus, and informed you how thoroughly I have experienced his worth, and how much I love him. Let me intreat you to honour him with your patronage in a way suitable to the generosity of your heart and the eminence of your station. But above all, admit him into a share of your affection; for though you were to confer upon him the utmost you have in your power to bestow, you can give him nothing so valuable as your friendship. That you may see he is worthy of it, even to the highest degree of intimacy, I have sent you this short sketch of his character. I should continue my intercessions in his behalf, but that I am sure you do not love to be pressed and I have already repeated them in every line of this letter; for to show a just reason for what one asks, is to intercede in the strongest manner. Farewell.

(To Calvisius)

I NEVER spent any time more agreeably, I think, than I did lately with Spurinna. I am so much pleased with the uninterrupted regularity of his way of life, that if ever I should arrive at old age, there is no man whom I would sooner choose for my model. I look upon order in human actions, especially at that advanced period, with the same sort of pleasure as I behold the settled course of the heavenly bodies. In youths, indeed, there is a certain irregularity and agitation by no means unbecoming; but in age, when business is unseasonable and ambition indecent, all should be calm and uniform.

This rule Spurinna religiously pursues throughout his whole conduct. Even in those transactions which one might call minute and inconsiderable did they not occur every day, he observes a certain periodical season and method. The first part of the morning he devotes to study; at eight he dresses and walks about three miles, in which he enjoys at once contemplation and exercise. At his return, if he has any friends with him in his house, he enters upon some polite and useful topic of conversation; if he is alone somebody reads to him; and sometimes too when he is not, if it is agreeable to his company. When this is over he reposes himself, and then again either takes up a book, or falls into some discourse even more entertaining and instructive. He afterwards takes the air in his chariot, either with his wife (who is a lady of uncommon merit) or with some friend: a happiness which lately was mine! — How agreeable, how noble is the enjoyment of him in that hour of privacy! You would fancy you were hearing some worthy of ancient times, inflaming your heart with the most heroic examples, and instructing your mind with the most exalted precepts: which yet he delivers with so modest an air, that there is not the least appearance of dictating in his conversation. When he has thus taken a tour of about seven miles, he gets out of his chariot and walks a mile more, after which he returns home, and either reposes himself, or retires to his study. He has an excellent taste for poetry, and composes in the lyric manner, both in Greek and Latin, with great judgment. It is surprising what an ease of spirit and gaiety runs through his verses, which the merit of the author renders still more valuable. When the baths are ready, which in winter is about three o'clock, and in summer about two, he undresses himself; and if there happens to be no wind, he walks for some time in the sun. After this he plays for a considerable time at tennis; for by this sort of exercise too, he combats the effects of old age. When he has bathed, he throws himself upon his couch till supper time, and in the meanwhile some agreeable and entertaining author is read to him. In this, as in all the rest, his friends are at full liberty to partake; or to employ themselves in any other manner more suitable to their taste. You sit down to an elegant yet frugal repast, which is served up in pure and antique plate. He has likewise a complete equipage for his side-board, in Corinthian metal, which is his pleasure, not his passion. At his table he is frequently entertained with comedians, that even his very amusements may be seasoned with good sense; and though he continues there, even in summer, till the night is something advanced, yet he prolongs the feast with so much affability and politeness, that none of his guests ever think it tedious. By this method of living he has preserved all his senses entire and his body active and vigorous to his seventy-eighth year, without discovering any appearance of old age, but the wisdom. This is a sort of life which I ardently aspire after; as I purpose to enjoy it, when I shall arrive at those years which will justify a retreat from business. In the meanwhile I am embarrassed with a thousand affairs, in which Spurinna is at once my support and my example. As long as it became him he entered into all the duties of public life.

It was by passing through the various offices of the state, by governing of provinces, and by indefatigable toil, that he merited the repose he now enjoys. I propose to myself the same course and the same end; and I give it to you under my hand that I do so. If an ill-timed ambition should carry me beyond it, produce this letter against me, and condemn me to repose, whenever I can enjoy it without being reproached with indolence. Farewell.

(To Fuscus)

YOU desire to know in what manner I dispose of my time in my summer villa at Tuscum. I rise just when I find myself in the humour, though generally with the sun; sometimes indeed sooner, but seldom later.

When I am up I continue to keep the shutters of my chamber-windows closed, as darkness and silence wonderfully promote meditation. Thus free and abstracted from those outward objects which dissipate attention, I am left to my own thoughts; nor suffer my mind to wander with my eyes in subjection to my mind, which, when they are not distracted by a multiplicity of external objects, see nothing but what the imagination represents to them. If I have any composition upon my hands, this is the time I choose to consider it, not only with respect to the general plan, but even the style and expression, which I settle and correct as if I were actually writing. In this manner I compose more or less as the subject is more or less difficult and I find myself able to retain it. Then I call my secretary, and opening the shutters, I dictate to him what I have composed, after which I dismiss him after a little while and then call him in again.

About ten or eleven of the clock (for I do not observe one fixed hour), according as the weather proves, I either walk upon my terrace, or in the covered portico, and there I continue to meditate or dictate what remains upon the subject in which I am engaged. From thence I get into my chariot, where I employ myself as before when I was walking or in my study; and find this changing of the scene preserves and enlivens my attention. At my return home, I repose myself; then I take a walk; and after that repeat aloud some Greek or Latin oration, not so much for the sake of strengthening my elocution as my digestion; though indeed the voice at the same time finds its account in this practice. Then I walk again and am anointed, take my exercises, and go into the bath. At supper, if I have only my wife or a few friends with me, some author is read to us; and after supper we are entertained either with music or an interlude. When that is finished, I take my walk with my family, in the number of which I am not without some persons of literature. Thus we pass our evenings in various conversation; and the day, even when it is at the longest, steals away imperceptibly.

Upon some occasions, I change the order in certain of the articles above mentioned. For instance, if I have studied longer or walked more than usual, after my second sleep and reading an oration or two aloud, instead of using my chariot I get on horseback; by which means I take as much exercise and lose less time. The visits of my friends from the neighbouring villages claim some part of the day; and sometimes, by an agreeable interruption, they come in very seasonably to relieve me when I am fatigued. I now and then amuse myself with sporting, but always take my tablets into the field, that though I should not meet with game, I may at least bring home something. Part of my time too (though not as much as they desire) is allotted to my tenants; and I find their rustic complaints give a zest to my studies and engagements of the polite kind. Farewell.

V

E. F.G.

Eight letters of Edward FitzGerald

I

(To W. F. Pollock)

GELDESTONE, *June* 24/42

DEAR POLLOCK, — There is that poor fellow Thackeray gone off to Ireland: and what a lazy beast I am for not going with him. But except for a journey of two days, I get as dull as dirt. I wish somebody had gone with him. But he will find lots of companions in Ireland. What is become of A. T.[1]? You never told me that, nor how his book went on: about which I have really a curiosity. I see the advertisement of Edwin the Fair in the papers: something about the Heptarchy, I suppose; a stupid time, whenever it was. And my dear Daddy's Tragedy [2] too, has any one read it?

We have been burnt up here, but to-day (the grass being just mowed) it rains pitchforks, which might be useful if not coming in such great numbers. But our garden is full of roses and all capital things. I wish

[1] Tennyson.

[2] Wordsworth's "The Borderers."

trade was going on well: and that we could be left as we are.

I have written a note to Spedding, such an one as he sent me, a ruffian; I have the pleasure of abusing some of his idols in it. A man on the coach the other day told me that all was being settled very easily in America, but stage-coach politicians are not always to be trusted. I propose that we leave Spedding as a hostage in the hands of the Americans. They must send over Willis or some one of their great men.

When do you set off on your trip to the Hebrides? or your yachting, wherever it is? I mean to go to Blenheim to see a Raffaelle this year, and that is all I propose to do. No sights recompense the often undoing and doing up of a carpet-bag. What then is the stamping down, strapping, and locking up of a trunk, with all the blood in your head! If one were rich, and travelled with a valet to do all, it would be well. The only other alternative is to travel with nothing but the clothes on one's back.

Sic cogitabat. — Yours ever, E. F.G.

II

(To S. Laurence)

Boulge, Woodbridge (*January* 30, 1848)

My dear Laurence, — How are you — how are you getting on? A voice from the tombs thus addresses you; respect the dead, and answer.

Barton is well; that is, I left him well on Friday; but he was just going off to attend a Quaker's funeral in the snow: whether he has survived that, I don't know.

To-morrow is his Birth-day: and I am going (if he be alive) to help him to celebrate it. His portrait has been hung (under my directions) over the mantel-piece in his sitting-room, with a broad margin of some red stuff behind it, to set it off. You may turn up your nose at all this; but let me tell you it is considered one of the happiest contrivances ever adopted in Woodbridge. Nineteen people out of twenty like the portrait much; the twentieth, you may be sure, is a man of no taste at all.

I hear you were for a long time in Cumberland. Did you paint a waterfall — or old Wordsworth — or Skiddaw, or any of the beauties? Did you see anything so inviting to the pencil as the river Deben? When are you coming to see us again? Churchyard relies on your coming; but then he is a very sanguine man, and, though a lawyer, wonderfully confident in the promises of men. How are all your family? You see I have asked you some questions; so you must answer them; and believe me yours truly, E. FitzGerald

III

(To Mrs. Cowell)

London, *Friday* (*April* 25, 1856)

My dear Lady, — The Picture after all did not go down yesterday as I meant, but shall and will go to-morrow (Saturday). Also I shall send you dear Major Moor's *Oriental Fragments;* an almost worthless Book, I doubt, to those who did not know him — which means, *love* him! And somehow all of us in our corner of Suffolk knew something of him: and so again loved something of him. For there was nothing at all about him not to be beloved. Ah! I think how interested he would have been with all this Persian: and how we should have disputed over parts and expressions over a glass of his Shiraz wine (for he had some) in his snug Parlour, or in his Cornfields when the Sun fell upon the latest Gleaners. He is dead! and you will go where he lived, to be dead to me!

Remember to take poor Barton's little Book with you to India; better than many a better Book to you there!

I got a glimpse of Professor Müller's Essay[1] — full of fine things; but I hardly gather it up into a good whole, which is very likely my fault; from hasty perusal, ignorance, or other Incapacity. Perhaps, on the other hand, he found the Subject too great for his Space; and so has left it disproportioned, which the German is not inapt to do. But one may be well thankful for such admirable fragments, perhaps left so in the very honesty that is above rounding them into a specious Theory which will not hold.

In a footnote to the foregoing letter Mr. Aldis Wright says: "In another letter written about the same time he (E. F.G.) says, 'The letter to Major Price at the beginning is worth any Money, and almost any Love.' This dedication by Major Moor to his old comrade in arms FitzGerald would sometimes try to read aloud, but would break down before he could finish it." I append it here: —

MY DEAR PRICE, — Accept the Dedication of this little Volume — a very trifling testimony of that Esteem and Friendship which have been growing uninterruptedly, not far short of half a century.

[1] Max Müller's "Essay on Comparative Mythology."

Our destinies have run nearly parallel over a considerable portion of the course of our lives. In early day we started as "Soldiers of Fortune" for the same country. So long ago as 1783 we were, though then unknown to each other, within gun-shot perhaps, in military operations against TIPPOO on the coast of *Malabar*. We have since served together in the same armies, the same detachments, the same garrisons, and the same regiments. We have together stormed the same forts — have been grievously maimed and mutilated in the service of our dearly beloved Country, and our blood has moistened the same dust.

After an active intertropical servitude of nearly a quarter of a century — having filled almost every staff situation of the same army; having gained the same military rank; we returned with an honorable competency resulting from persevering industry and economy, to our native Country, on the same ship; and have set up our several resting-places within sight of our native hills. Unwilling to be altogether idle or useless, we alike share in the administration of the Justice, and in the preservation of the Peace, of our respective Counties, by acting in various Commissions under the Crown.

Not unobservant while in *India* of the people among whom our early fortunes cast us, or of their languages or literature, we have, since our return, during the lapse of another quarter of a century, resorted to the Press; and have published to our Countrymen the results of such observances — with this difference, — that yours have been chiefly directed to *Mahommedan*, mine to *Hindu* literature: and with this farther difference; — that you have made the most of the advantages of a good and classical education, while I have had to contend with the disadvantages of a bad one. You have drank deep, while I have only sipped at those Oriental Literary springs.

They who live long must pay the sad penalties of existence: — must see their old comrades, and associates, and friends, fall around them. If we look back for our early brethren in arms — where are they? And more and more recently we are called to mourn over the ripened Affections of our later years. It behoves us therefore to rivet the more closely the remaining links of Friendship's early chain — and to await, in contentedness and humble hope, its final severance.

With these sentiments and feelings towards you, My dear PRICE, my oldest FELLOW SOLDIER and FRIEND, I most cordially and affectionately say FAREWELL.

EDWARD MOOR

BEALINGS, SUFFOLK
March 1, 1834

IV

(To George Crabbe)

MARKET HILL, WOODBRIDGE
Monday (*March* 10, 1862)

MY DEAR GEORGE, — There is Farlingay left in applepie order, with its good Servants, Gardener, etc., as old Smith left them, and I am asked to take it as it is: and yet — I am afraid to leave the poor Town with its little bustle! As one grows older, lonelier, and sadder, is not the little Town best, though Farlingay be the Pink of Places?

I have bought a new Boat, which is not yet from London: and am altering (and I doubt spoiling) my old one, just when I did not want to meddle with it at all. Then, in a sudden fit, I sold out all my Bank Stock into Dutch Funds, which won't give me as much Income; my only consolation being that, directly after I had done it, the Bank Clerk (here) rushed out from his Desk to assure me Bank Stock had fallen because a smaller Dividend is expected. I believe I am now more considered in the Town, as having exhibited this foreknowledge.

The "Town Hall" is being decorated with Flags, etc., for the Odd Fellows Dinner, which comes off To-day. But the Town itself is distracted with the Question as to where the New School shall be; Bishop Taylor having persuaded the Inspector to choose Land near his (the Bishop's) Estate down in the lower Part of the Town (at foot of the sandhill). So the Bishop walks about enveloped in his virtue, and proof against all unchristian malevolence.

I have been in my glory tearing up 20 Volumes of the Gentleman's Magazine to get out Scraps of Mitford and Green's Diary, of which I make Volumes, and then call them my Works.

I have hung my Pictures, which are spoilt by a vile Paper.

V

(To W. F. Pollock)

MARKET HILL, WOODBRIDGE
October 28 (1867)

NOW, my dear Pollock, I have put on a new Goose-quill Nib, on purpose to write my best MS to you. But the new Nib has very little to say for me: the old

Story: dodging about in my Ship for these last five months: indeed during all that time not having lain, I believe, for three consecutive Nights in Christian Sheets. But now all that is over: this very day is my little Ship being dismantled, and to-morrow will she go up to her middle in mud, and here am I anchored to my old Desk for the Winter; and beginning, as usual, to write to my Friends, to tell them what little there is to tell of myself, and asking them to tell what they can of themselves in return. I shall even fire a shot at old Spedding; who would not answer my last Letters at all: innocent as they were, I am sure: and asking definite Questions, which he once told me he required if I wanted any Answer. I suppose he is now in Cumberland. What *is* become of Bacon? Are you one of the Converted, who go the whole Hog?

Thompson — no, I mean the Master of Trinity — has replied to my half-yearly Enquiries in a very kind Letter. He tells me that my friend Edward Cowell has pleased all the Audience he had with an inaugural Lecture about Sanskrit. Also, that there is such an Article in the Quarterly about the Talmud as has not been seen (so fine an Article, I mean) for years.

I have had Don Quixote, Boccaccio, and my dear Sophocles (once more) for company on board: the first of these so delightful, that I got to love the very Dictionary in which I had to look out the words: yes, and often the same words over and over again. The Book really seemed to me the most delightful of all Books: Boccaccio, delightful too, but millions of miles behind; in fact, a whole Planet away.

VI

(To W. F. Pollock)

WOODBRIDGE, *November* 11 (1867)

MY DEAR POLLOCK, — I must thank you for your Letter — good Fellow as you were to write it. I must say that you never leave one long in doubt as to whether one is any longer acceptable or not.

Not like that Wretch Spedding; who, since I wrote you, did write to me at last, and confessed that he slightly repented of not writing before. However, I am contented that he thinks it worth while to think twice about the matter. He now talks about two more Volumes of Bacon in the Spring: and then he says he will take the reins into his own hands, and publish Volume by Volume as it is finished. He is now *entêté* (I forget how it's spelt) about some sort of Phonetic Alphabet.

I have not yet revived my appetite for Novels: not even for my dear "Woman in White": which I should like to have read to me; and which even now exerts a sort of magnetism in drawing me toward the corner of a dark Cupboard, or Closet, in which (like the proprietary Skeleton) she lies.

I have heard from *Mrs.* Alfred, who (as you may know) answers for Husband and Self. She does not give a good Account of one Son (I believe the Eldest): and Frederic Tennyson, who was at Farringford this Autumn, thinks them both very delicate. Is it to be with A. T., as is said to be the Fate of your great Men: to leave no Posterity?

Well — and I have heard from the Master of Trinity,

who encloses me a Leaf of Proof-sheet of Plato, with good English Notes, corrected, and therefore, I doubt not, written by himself. The Page he encloses is meant to answer a Question I put to him years ago. I don't know when, nor on what occasion. However, I find the Question is left ambiguous even by Scholars.

Are you overrun in London with "Champagne Charlie is my Name"? A brutal Thing; nearly worthless — the Tune, I mean — but yet not quite — else it would not become so great a Bore. No: I can see, to my Sorrow, that it has some Go — which Mendelssohn had not. But Mozart, Rossini, and Handel had. I can't help thinking that Opera will have to die for a time: certainly there seems to be no new Blood to keep it alive: and the Old Works of Genius want rest. I have never heard Faust: only Bits — which I suppose were thought the best Bits. They were expressive — musically ingenious, etc. — but the part of Hamlet — the one Divine Soul of Music, Melody — was not there. I think that such a Fuss can be made about it only because there is nothing better.

VII

(To E. B. Cowell)

WOODBRIDGE, *March* 1/69

MY DEAR COWELL, — . . . My Lugger Captain has just left me to go on his Mackerel Voyage to the Western Coast; and I don't know when I shall see him again. Just after he went, a muffled bell from the Church here began to toll for somebody's death: it sounded like a Bell under the sea. He sat listening to the Hymn played by the Church chimes last evening, and said he could hear it all as if in Lowestoft Church when he was a Boy, "Jesus our Deliverer"! You can't think what a grand, tender Soul this is, lodged in a suitable carcase.

VIII

(To Fanny Kemble)

WOODBRIDGE, *October* 17, 1882

MY DEAR MRS. KEMBLE, — I suppose that you are returned from the Loire by this time; but as I am not sure that you have returned to the "Hotel des Deux Mondes" whence you dated your last, I make bold once more to trouble Coutts with adding your Address to my Letter. I think I shall have it from yourself not long after. I shall like to hear a word about my old France, dear to me from childish associations, and in particular of the Loire, endeared to me by Sévigné; for I never saw the glimmer of its waters myself. . . .

It seems to me (but I believe it seems so every year) that our trees keep their leaves very long; I suppose, because of no severe frosts or winds up to this time. And my garden still shows some Geranium, Salvia, Nasturtium, Great Convolvulus, and that grand African Marigold whose Colour is so comfortable to us Spanish-like Paddies. I have also a dear Oleander which even now has a score of blossoms on it, and touches the top of my little Green-house; having been sent me when "haut comme ça," as Marquis Somebody used to say in the days of Louis XIV. Don't you love the Oleander? So clean in its leaves and stem, and so beautiful in its flower; loving to stand in water which it drinks up so fast. I rather worship mine.

VI

ELIA

I

The Failure of Godwin's Play

December 16, 1800

WE are damn'd!

Not the facetious epilogue could save us. For as the editor of the "Morning Post," quick-sighted gentleman! hath this morning truly observed (I beg pardon if I falsify his *words*, their profound *sense* I am sure I retain), both prologue and epilogue were worthy of accompanying such a piece; and indeed (mark the profundity, Mister Manning) were received with proper indignation by such of the audience only as thought either worth attending to. PROFESSOR, thy glories wax dim! Again, the incomparable author of the "True Briton" declareth in *his* paper (bearing same date) that the epilogue was an indifferent attempt at humour and character, and failed in both. I forbear to mention the other papers, because I have not read them. O PROFESSOR, how different thy feelings now (*quantum mutatus ab illo professore, qui in agris philosophiæ tantas victorias aquisivisti*), — how different thy proud feelings but one little week ago, — thy anticipation of thy nine nights, — those visionary claps, which have soothed thy soul by day and thy dreams by night! Calling in accidentally on the Professor while he was out, I was ushered into the study; and my nose quickly (most sagacious always) pointed me to four tokens lying loose upon thy table, Professor, which indicated thy violent and satanical pride of heart. Imprimis, there caught mine eye a list of six persons, thy friends, whom thou didst meditate inviting to a sumptuous dinner on the Thursday, anticipating the profits of thy Saturday's play to answer charges; I was in the honoured file! Next, a stronger evidence of thy violent and almost satanical pride, lay a list of all the morning papers (from the "Morning Chronicle" downwards to the "Porcupine,") with the places of their respective offices, where thou wast meditating to insert, and didst insert, an elaborate sketch of the story of thy play — stones in thy enemy's hand to bruise thee with; and severely wast thou bruised, O Professor! nor do I know what oil to pour into thy wounds. Next, which convinced me to a dead conviction of thy pride, violent and almost satanical pride — lay a list of books, which thy un-tragedy-favoured pocket could never answer; Dodsley's Old Plays, Malone's Shakspeare (still harping upon thy play, thy philosophy abandoned meanwhile to Christians and superstitious minds); nay, I believe (if I can believe my memory), that the ambitious Encyclopædia itself was part of thy meditated acquisitions; but many a playbook was there. All these visions are *damned;* and thou, Professor, must read Shakspere in future out of a common edition; and, hark ye, pray read him to a little better purpose! Last and strongest against thee (in colours manifest as the hand upon Belshazzar's wall), lay a volume of poems by C. Lloyd and C. Lamb. Thy heart misgave thee, that thy assistant might possibly not have talent enough to furnish thee an epilogue! Manning, all these things came over my mind; all the gratulations that would have thickened upon him, and even some have glanced aside upon his humble friend; the vanity, and the fame, and the profits (the Professor is £500 ideal money out of pocket by this failure, besides £200 he would have got for the copyright, and the Professor is never much beforehand with the world; what he gets is all by the sweat of his brow and dint of brain, for the Professor, though a sure man, is also a slow); and now to muse upon thy altered physiognomy, thy pale and squalid appearance (a kind of *blue sickness* about the eyelids), and thy crest fallen, and thy proud demand of £200 from thy bookseller changed to an uncertainty of his taking it at all, or giving thee full £50. The Professor has won my heart by this *his* mournful catastrophe. You remember Marshall, who dined with him at my house; I met him in the lobby immediately after the damnation of the Professor's play, and he looked to me like an angel: his face was lengthened, and ALL OVER SWEAT; I never saw such a care-fraught visage; I could have hugged him, I loved him so intensely. "From every pore of him a perfume fell." I have seen that man in many situations, and from my soul I think that a more god-like honest soul exists not in this world. The Professor's poor nerves trembling with the recent shock, he hurried him away to my house to supper; and there we comforted him as well as we could. He came to consult me about a change of catastrophe; but alas! the piece was condemned long before that crisis. I at first humoured him with a specious proposition, but have since joined his true friends in advising him to give it up. He did it with a pang, and is to print it as *his*. L.

II

Brawn

16 Mitre-Court Buildings
Saturday, February 24 [*i.e.* 23], 1805

DEAR MANNING, — I have been very unwell since I saw you. A sad depression of spirits, a most unaccountable nervousness; from which I have been partially relieved by an odd accident. You knew Dick Hopkins, the swearing scullion of Caius? This fellow, by industry and agility, has thrust himself into the important situations (no sinecures, believe me) of cook to Trinity Hall and Caius College: and the generous creature has contrived with the greatest delicacy imaginable, to send me a present of Cambridge brawn. What makes it the more extraordinary is, that the man never saw me in his life that I know of. I suppose he has *heard* of me. I did not immediately recognise the donor; but one of Richard's cards, which had accidentally fallen into the straw, detected him in a moment. Dick, you know, was always remarkable for flourishing. His card imports, that "orders (to wit, for brawn), from any part of England, Scotland, or Ireland, will be duly executed," etc. At first, I thought of declining the present; but Richard knew my blind side when he pitched upon brawn. 'Tis of all my hobbies the supreme in the eating way. He might have sent sops from the pan, skimmings, crumplets, chips, hog's lard, the tender brown judiciously scalped from a fillet of veal (dexterously replaced by a salamander), the tops of asparagus, fugitive livers, runaway gizzards of fowls, the eyes of martyred pigs, tender effusions of laxative woodcocks, the red spawn of lobsters, leverets' ears, and such pretty filchings common to cooks; but these had been ordinary presents, the everyday courtesies of dishwashers to their sweethearts. Brawn was a noble thought. It is not every common gullet-fancier that can properly esteem it. It is like a picture of one of the choice old Italian masters. Its gusto is of that hidden sort. As Wordsworth sings of a modest poet, — "you must love him, ere to you he will seem worthy of your love;" so brawn, you must taste it, ere to you it will seem to have any taste at all. But 'tis nuts to the adept: those that will send out their tongues and feelers to find it out. It will be wooed, and not unsought be won. Now, ham-essence, lobsters, turtle, such popular minions, absolutely *court you*, lay themselves out to strike you at first smack, like one of David's pictures (they call him *Darveed*), compared with the plain russet-coated wealth of a Titian or a Correggio, as I illustrated above. Such are the obvious glaring heathen virtues of a corporation dinner, compared with the reserved collegiate worth of brawn. Do me the favour to leave off the business which you may be at present upon, and go immediately to the kitchens of Trinity and Caius, and make my most respectful compliments to Mr. Richard Hopkins, and assure him that his brawn is most excellent; and that I am moreover obliged to him for his innuendo about salt water and bran, which I shall not fail to improve. I leave it to you whether you shall choose to pay him the civility of asking him to dinner while you stay in Cambridge, or in whatever other way you may best like to show your gratitude to *my friend.* Richard Hopkins, considered in many points of view, is a very extraordinary character. Adieu: I hope to see you to supper in London soon, where we will taste Richard's brawn, and drink his health in a cheerful but moderate cup. We have not many such men in any rank of life as Mr. R. Hopkins. Crisp the barber, of St. Mary's was just such another. I wonder *he* never sent me any little token, some chestnuts, or a puff, or two pound of hair just to remember him by; gifts are like nails. *Præsens ut absens*, that is, your *present* makes amends for your absence. — Yours,

C. LAMB

III

All the news, for China

March 28, 1809

DEAR MANNING, — I sent you a long letter by the ships which sailed the beginning of last month, accompanied with books, etc. Since I last wrote, Holcroft is dead. He died on Thursday last. So there is one of your friends whom you will never see again! Perhaps the next fleet may bring you a letter from Martin Burney, to say that he writes by desire of Miss Lamb, who is not well enough to write herself, to inform you that her brother died on Thursday last, 14th June, etc. But I hope *not*. I should be sorry to give occasion to open a correspondence between Martin and you. This letter must be short, for I have driven it off to the very moment of doing up the packets; and besides, that which I refer to above is a very long one; and if you have received my books, you will have enough to do to read them. While I think on it, let me tell you we are moved. Don't come any more to Mitre Court Buildings. We are at 34 Southampton Buildings, Chancery Lane, and shall be here till about the end of May: then we remove to No. 4 Inner Temple Lane, where I mean to live and die; for I have such horror of moving, that I would not take a benefice from the King, if I was not indulged with non-residence. What a dislocation of comfort is comprised in that word moving! Such a heap of little nasty things, after you think all is got into the cart: old dredging-boxes, worn-out brushes, gallipots, vials, things that it is impossible the most necessitous person can ever want, but which the women, who preside on these occasions, will not leave behind if it was to save your soul; they'd keep the cart ten minutes to stow in dirty pipes and broken matches, to show their economy. Then you can find nothing you want for many days after you get into your new lodgings. You must comb your hair with your fingers, wash your hands without soap, go about in dirty gaiters. Was I Diogenes, I would not move out of a kilderkin into a hogshead, though the first had had nothing but small beer in it, and the second reeked claret. Our place of final destination, — I don't mean the grave, but No. 2 [4] Inner Temple Lane, — looks out upon a gloomy churchyard-like court, called Hare Court, with three trees and a pump in it. Do you know it? I was born near it, and used to drink at that pump when I was a Rechabite of six years old. If you see newspapers you will read about Mrs. Clarke. The sensation in London about this nonsensical business is marvellous. I remember nothing in my life like it. Thousands of ballads, caricatures, lives, of Mrs. Clarke, in every blind alley. Yet in the midst of this stir, a sublime abstracted dancing-master, who attends a family we know in Kensington, being asked a question about the progress of the examination in the House, inquired who Mrs. Clarke was? He had heard nothing of it. He had evaded this omnipresence by utter insignificancy! The Duke should make that man his confidential valet. I proposed locking him up, barring him the use of his fiddle and red pumps, until he had minutely perused and committed to memory the whole body of the examinations, which employed the House of Commons a fortnight, to teach him to be more attentive to what concerns the public. I think I told you of Godwin's little book, and of Coleridge's prospectus, in my last; if I did not, remind me of it, and I will send you them, or an account of them, next fleet. I have no conveniency of doing it by this. Mrs. —— [1] grows every day in disfavour with God and man. I will be buried with this inscription over me: — "Here lies C. L., the Woman-hater" — I mean that hated ONE WOMAN: for the rest, God bless them, and when he makes any more, make 'em prettier. How do you like the Mandarinesses? Are you on some little footing with any of them? This is Wednesday. On Wednesdays is my levee. The Captain, Martin, Phillips (not the Sheriff), Rickman, and some more, are constant attendants, besides stray visitors. We play at whist, eat cold meat and hot potatoes, and any gentleman that chooses smokes. Why do you never drop in? You'll come some day, won't you?

C. LAMB, etc.

[1] Probably Mrs. Godwin.

IV

Tommy Bye

May 28, 1819

MY DEAR M[ANNING],— I want to know how your brother is, if you have heard lately. I want to know about you. I wish you were nearer. How are my cousins, the Gladmans of Wheathamstead, and farmer Bruton? Mrs. Bruton is a glorious woman.

Hail, Mackery End —

This is a fragment of a blank verse poem which I once meditated, but got no further. The E. I. H. has been thrown into a quandary by the strange phenomenon of poor Tommy Bye, whom I have known man and madman twenty-seven years, he being elder here than myself by nine years and more. He was always a pleasant, gossiping, half-headed, muzzy, dozing, dreaming, walk-about, inoffensive chap; a little too fond of the creature — who isn't at times? — but Tommy had not brains to work off an over-night's surfeit by ten o'clock next morning, and unfortunately, in he wandered the other morning drunk with last night, and with a superfœtation of drink taken in since he set out from bed. He came staggering under his double burthen, like trees in Java, bearing at once blossom, fruit, and falling fruit, as I have heard you or some other traveller tell, with his face literally as blue as the bluest firmament; some wretched calico that he had mopped his poor oozy front with had rendered up its native dye, and the devil a bit would he consent to wash it, but swore was it characteristic, for he was going to the sale of indigo, and set up a laugh which I did not think the lungs of mortal man were competent to. It was like a thousand people laughing, or the Goblin Page. He imagined afterwards that the whole office had been laughing at him, so strange did his own sounds strike upon his *non*sensorium. But Tommy has laughed his last laugh, and awoke the next day to find himself reduced from an abused income of £600 per annum to one-sixth of the sum, after thirty-six years' tolerably good service. The quality of mercy was not strained in his behalf; the gentle dews dropt not on him from heaven. It just came across me that I was writing to Canton. How is Ball? "Mr. B. is a P——." Will you drop in to-morrow night? Fanny Kelly is coming, if she does not cheat us. Mrs. *Gold* is well, but proves "uncoined," as the lovers about Wheathampstead would say.

O hard hearted Burrell
With teeth like a squirrel —

I have not had such a quiet half hour to sit down to a quiet letter for many years. I have not been interrupted above four times. I wrote a letter the other day in alternate lines, black ink and red, and you cannot think how it chilled the flow of ideas. Next Monday is Whit-Monday. What a reflection! Twelve years ago, and I should have kept that and the following holiday in the fields a-Maying. All of those pretty pastoral delights are over. This dead, everlasting dead desk — how it weighs the spirit of a gentleman down! This dead wood of the desk instead of your living trees! But then, again, I hate the Joskins, *a name for Hertfordshire bumpkins.* Each state of life has its inconvenience; but then, again, mine has more than one. Not that I repine, or grudge, or murmur at my destiny. I have meat and drink, and decent apparel; I shall, at least, when I get a new hat.

A red-haired man has just interrupted me. He has broke the current of my thoughts. I haven't a word to add. I don't know why I send this letter, but I have had a hankering to hear about you some days. Perhaps it will go off before your reply comes. If it don't, I assure you no letter was ever welcomer from you, from Paris or Macao. C. LAMB

V

The Little Pig

(To S. T. Coleridge)

March 9, 1822

DEAR C., — It gives me great satisfaction to hear that the pig turned out so well — they are interesting creatures at a certain age — what a pity such buds should blow out into the maturity of rank bacon! You had all some of the crackling — and brain sauce — did you remember to rub it with butter, and gently dredge it a little, just before the crisis? Did the eyes come away kindly with no Œdipean avulsion? Was the crackling the colour of the ripe pomegranate? Had you no complement of boiled neck of mutton before it, to blunt the edge of delicate desire? Did you flesh maiden teeth in it? Not that I sent the pig, or can form the remotest guess what part Owen could play in the business. I never knew him give anything away in my life. He would not begin with strangers. I suspect the pig, after all, was meant for me; but at the unlucky juncture of time being absent, the present somehow went round to Highgate. To confess an honest truth, a pig is one of those things I could never think of sending away. Teals, wigeons, snipes, barn-door fowl, ducks, geese — your tame villatic things — Welsh mutton, collars of brawn, sturgeon, fresh or pickled, your potted char, Swiss cheeses, French pies, early grapes, muscadines, I impart as freely unto my friends as to myself. They are but self-extended; but pardon me if I stop somewhere — where the fine feeling of benevolence giveth a higher smack than the sensual rarity — there my friends (or any good man) may command me; but pigs are pigs, and I myself therein am nearest to myself. Nay, I should think it an affront, an undervaluing done to Nature who bestowed such a boon upon me, if in a churlish mood I parted with the precious gift. One of the bitterest pangs of remorse I ever felt was when a child — when my kind old aunt had strained her pocket-strings to bestow a sixpenny whole plum-cake upon me. In my way home through the Borough, I met a venerable old man, not a mendicant, but thereabouts — a look-beggar, not a verbal petitionist; and in the coxcombry of taught-charity I gave away the cake to him. I walked on a little in all the pride of an Evangelical peacock, when of a sudden my old aunt's kindness crossed me — the sum it was to her — the pleasure she had a right to expect that I — not the old impostor — should take in eating her cake — the cursed ingratitude by which, under the colour of a Christian virtue, I had frustrated her cherished purpose. I sobbed, wept, and took it to heart so grievously, that I think I never suffered the like — and I was right. It was a piece of unfeeling hypocrisy, and proved a lesson to me ever after. The cake has long been masticated, consigned to dunghill with the ashes of that unseasonable pauper.

But when Providence, who is better to us all than our aunts, gives me a pig, remembering my temptation and my fall, I shall endeavour to act towards it more in the spirit of the donor's purpose.

Yours (short of pig) to command in everything.

C. L.

VI

The Toast

(To Miss Hutchinson)

APROPOS of birds — the other day at a large dinner, being call'd upon for a toast, I gave, as the best toast I knew, "Wood-cock toast," which was drunk with 3 cheers. — Yours affect'ly,

C. LAMB

VII

Sunday

(To J. B. Dibdin)

An answer is requested.

[P.M. *September* 9, 1826]

Saturday

DEAR D[IBDIN], — I have observed that a Letter is never more acceptable than when received upon a rainy day, especially a rainy Sunday; which moves me to send you somewhat, however short. This will find you sitting after Breakfast, which you will have prolonged as far as you can with consistency to the poor handmaid that has the reversion of the Tea Leaves; making two nibbles of your last morsel of *stale* roll (you cannot have hot new ones on the Sabbath), and reluctantly coming to an end, because when that is done, what can you do till dinner? You cannot go to the Beach, for the rain is drowning the sea, turning rank Thetis fresh, taking the brine out of Neptune's pickles, while mermaids sit upon rocks with umbrellas, their ivory combs sheathed for spoiling in the wet of waters foreign to them. You cannot go to the library, for it's shut. You are not religious enough to go to church. O it is worth while to cultivate piety to the gods, to have something to fill the heart up on a wet Sunday! You cannot cast accounts, for your ledger is being eaten up with moths in the Ancient Jewry. You cannot play at draughts, for there is none to play with you, and besides there is not a draught-board in the house. You cannot go to market, for it closed last night. You cannot look in to the shops, their backs are shut upon you. You cannot read the Bible, for it is not good reading for the sick and the hypochondriacal. You cannot while away an hour with a friend, for you have no friend round that Wrekin. You cannot divert yourself with a stray acquaintance, for you have picked none up. You cannot bear the chiming of Bells, for they invite you to a banquet, where you are no visitant. You cannot cheer yourself with the prospect of a to-morrow's letter, for none come on Mondays. You cannot count those endless vials on the mantlepiece with any hope of making a variation in their numbers. You have counted your spiders: your Bastile is exhausted. You sit and deliberately curse your hard exile from all familiar sights and sounds. Old Ranking poking in his head unexpectedly would just now be as good to you as Grimaldi. Any thing to deliver you from this intolerable weight of Ennui. You are too ill to shake it off: not ill enough to submit to it, and to lie down as a lamb under it. The Tyranny of Sickness is nothing to the Cruelty of Convalescence: 'tis to have Thirty Tyrants for one. That pattering rain drops on your brain. You'll be worse after dinner, for you must dine at one to-day, that Betty may go to afternoon service. She insists upon having her chopped hay. And then when she goes out, who *was* something to you, something to speak to — what an interminable afternoon you'll have to go thro'. You can't break yourself from your locality: you cannot say "To-morrow morning I set off for Banstead, by God": for you are book'd for Wednesday. Foreseeing this, I thought a *cheerful letter* would come in opportunely. If any of the little topics for mirth I have thought upon should serve you in this utter extinguishment of sunshine, to make you a little merry, I shall have had my ends. I love to make things comfortable. [*Here is an erasure.*] This, which is scratch'd out, was the most material thing I had to say. But on maturer thoughts I defer it.

P.S. — We are just sitting down to dinner with a pleasant party, Coleridge, Reynolds the dramatist, and Sam Bloxam: to-morrow (that is, to-*day*), Liston, and Wyat of the Wells, dine with us. May this find you as jolly and freakish as we mean to be.

C. Lamb

VII

RURAL FELICITY

Thomas Gray tells the Rev. James Brown of chaos and cream

Old Park, *July* 19, 1762

DEAR SIR, — After my fortnight's residence at York, I am arrived here. The Precentor is very hopefully improved in dignity. His scarf sets the fullest about his ears; his surplice has the most the air of lawn-sleeves you can imagine in so short a time; he begins to complain of qualms and indigestions from repose and repletion: in short, *il tranche du Prelat.* We went twice a-day to church with our vergers and all our pomp. Here the scene is totally altered: we breakfast at six in the morning, and go to bed at ten. The house rings all days with carpenters and upholsterers, and without doors we swarm with labourers and builders. The books are not yet unpacked, and there is but one pen in the house. Jetty and Fadge (two favourite sows) are always coming into the entry, and there is a concert of poultry under every window: we take in no newspaper or magazine, but the cream and butter is beyond compare. You are wished for every day, and you may imagine how acceptable a correspondent you must be. Pray write soon, and believe me ever sincerely yours, T. G.

Rural Felicity

Thomas Gray provides Wharton with a garden calendar

SATURDAY, *July* 21, 1759

DEAR DOCTOR, — I have at last found rest for the sole of my gouty foot in your old dining-room, and hope in spite of the damnation denounced by the bishop's two chaplains, that you may find at least an equal satisfaction and repose at Old Park. If your bog prove as comfortable as my oven, I shall see no occasion to pity you; and only wish that you may *brew* no worse than I *bake*. You totally mistake my talents, when you impute to me any magical skill in planting roses. I know, I am no conjuror in these things; when they are done, I can find no fault, and that is all. Now this is the very reverse of genius, and I feel my own littleness. Reasonable people know themselves better than is commonly imagined; and therefore (though I never saw any instance of it) I believe Mason, when he tells me he understands planting better than anything whatever. The *prophetic eye of taste* (as Mr. Pitt call'd it) sees all the beauties that a place is susceptible of, long before they are born; and when it plants a seedling, already sits under the shadow of it, and enjoys the effect it will have from every point of view that lies in prospect. You must therefore invoke Caractacus, and he will send his spirits from the top of Snowden to Cross Fell or Warden Law.

The thermometer is in the passage window (where the sun never comes) near the head of the back stairs. Since you went, I have never observed it lower than 68, most part of the day at 74, and yesterday at 5 in the afternoon it was at 79, the highest I have ever seen it. It now is prepared to correspond regularly with you at the hours you mention. The weather for this fortnight has been broiling without interruption, one thunder-shower excepted, which did not cool the air at all. Rye (I am told) is begun to be cut near London. In Cambridgeshire a fortnight ago the promise of harvest was the finest I ever saw, but the farmers complain (I hear) that the ears do not fill for want of wet. The wheat was then turning yellow. Duke-cherries are over in London; three days ago they sold for half-a-crown a pound. Caroons and Blackhearts very large and fine drive about the streets in wheel-barrows a penny a pound. Raspberries a few are yet remaining, but in a manner over. Melons are ripe, and apricots and Orleans-plums are to be seen in the fruit-shops. Roses are (I think) over a week ago. The jessamine (at Mrs. Dod's, on a S.W. wall) was in full bloom (if you remember) long before you went from hence, and so it continues. That below in the garden on a N.E. wall has been all this week covered in flowers. My nosegays from Covent Garden consist of nothing but scarlet martagons, everlasting-peas, double-stocks, pinks and flowering marjoram. As I have kept no exact account hitherto this year, I can say no more of July, that now is. Therefore, I shall annex one for the year 1754, which I observed day by day at Stoke. Observe, it had been then a cold rainy summer.

The heat was very moderate this month, and a great deal of rain fell. The sown hay was all got in by the first day, but the meadow-hay was not before the 23rd. It was very good and in plenty, but sold at 40 shillings a load in the field on account of the scarcity the year preceding. Barley was in the ear on the first day; grey and white peas in bloom. The bean flowers were going off. Duke-cherries in plenty on the 5th; hearts were also ripe. Green melons on the 6th, but watry and not sweet. Currants begun to ripen on the 8th, and red gooseberries had changed colour; tares were then in flower, and meadow-hay cutting. Lime-trees in full bloom on the 9th. Mushroom in perfection on the 17th. Wheat and oats had changed colour, and buck-wheat was in bloom on the 19th. The vine had then opened its blossoms, and the end of the month grapes were near the size of small peas. Turnips appeared above ground on the 22nd; and potatoes were in flower. Barley had changed its hue, and rye was almost ripe on the 23rd. The pineapple-strawberry was then in perfection. Black caroons were ripe, and some duke-cherries still remained on walls the 26th, but the hearts were then all spoiled by rain. Gooseberries red and white were then ripe, and currants in abundance.

On the 1st
Haws, turned red
Honey-suckles, in full bloom
Broomflower went off

On the 2nd
Phlomis, or yellow-tree-sage

On the 3rd
Virginia flowering Raspberry, blew
Shrub cinque-foil
Spiræa-frutex
Syringa went off

On the 7th
Balm of Gilead blowing

On the 8th
Common Jasmine blew
Moss-Provence Rose
Yellow and Austrian Roses go off

On the 9th
Yellow Jasmine blows
White, and Gum Cistus
Tamarisk in flower
Coccygria
Virginia-Sumach
Tutsan, or Park-leaves
Spanish-Broom
Scarlet, and painted Geraniums

On the 11th
Pyracantha, in berry
Mountain-Ash
White-Beam
Orange flowering
Winter Cherry

On the 15th
Single Velvet Rose goes off

On the 22nd
Lavender and Morjoram blow

On the 26th
Damask, red, moss, and double Velvet, Roses go off

On the 28th
Rosa-Mundi, and Rose without Thorns, go off

On the 31st
White Rose goes off

These were all the flowering Shrubs observed by me

GARDEN FLOWERS

On the 2nd
Convolvus Minor blows
Garden Poppy
Single Rose Campion
Double Larkspur
Candy Tuft
Common Marigold
Pansies continue blowing

On the 5th
Lupins blew, and white blow
Purple Toads-flax
White, and blue Campanula

On the 9th
Double-scarlet Lychnis blows
Tree Primrose
White Lilly
Willow-Bay
Scarlet Bean
French Marigold

On the 11th
Yellow Lupin blows
Tree-Mallow
Amaranthus Cat's-tail

On the 19th
Striped Lilly blows
Fairchild's Mule
Double rose-Campion
African Ragwort

On the 23rd
Whole Carnations blow

On the 24th
Double-white Stock in bloom

In the Fields Scabious, St. John's Wort, Trefoil, Yarrow, Bugloss, Purple Vetch, Wild-thyme, Pale Wood-Orchis, Betony, and white Clover, flowering on the 1st. Large blue Cranesbill the 9th; Ragwort, Mothmullein, and Brambles, the 20th; Knapweed all the month. There was rain (more or less) 13 days out of 31, this month; and 17 days out of 30 in June preceding

I was too late for the post on Saturday, so I continue on Monday. It is now 6 in the afternoon, and the thermometer is mounted to 80, though the wind is at N.E. by N. The gay Lady Essex is dead of a fever during her lying-in; and Mrs. Charles York last week, with one of her children, of the sore throat. Heberden, and (I think) Taylor, attended her; the latter had pronounced her out of danger; but Heberden doubted her. The little boy was at Acton, and escaped the infection.

Everybody continues as quiet about the invasion, as if a Frenchman, as soon as he set his foot on our coast, would die, like a toad in Ireland. Yet the king's tents and equipage are ordered to be ready at an hour's warning. Nobody knows, positively, what is the damage that Rodney has done, whether much or little: he can only guess himself; and the French have kept their own secret, as yet. Of the 12 millions, raised for the year, eight are gone already, and the old party assure us, there is no more to be had for next year. You may easily guess at the source of my intelligence, and therefore will not talk of it. News is hourly expected of a battle in Westphalia, for Pr. Ferdinand was certainly preparing to fight the French, who have taken Minden by storm.

I hear the D. of N. is much broke ever since his sister Castlecomer died: not that he cared for her, or saw her above once a year; but she was the last of the brood, that was left; and he now goes regularly to church, which he never did before. Adieu. I am ever yours.

I hope Mrs. Wharton's native air will be more civil to her, when they are better acquainted: my best compliments to her. I am glad the children are well.

William Cowper records his history as a gardener

(To Mrs King)

WESTON UNDERWOOD
October 11, 1788

MY DEAR MADAM, — You are perfectly secure from all danger of being overwhelmed with presents from me.

It is not much that a poet can possibly have it in his power to give. When he has presented his own works, he may be supposed to have exhausted all means of donation.

They are his only superfluity.

There was a time, but that time was before I commenced writer for the press, when I amused myself in a way somewhat similar to yours; allowing, I mean, for the difference between masculine and feminine operations.

The scissors and the needle are your chief implements; mine were the chisel and the saw.

In those days you might have been in some danger of too plentiful a return for your favours. Tables, such as they were, and joint stools such as never were, might have travelled to Pertenhall in most inconvenient abundance.

But I have long since discontinued this practice, and many others which I found it necessary to adopt, that I might escape the worst of all evils, both in itself and in its consequences — an idle life.

Many arts I have exercised with this view, for which nature never designed me, though among them were some in which I arrived at considerable proficiency, by mere dint of the most heroic perseverance. There is not a 'squire in all this country who can boast of having made better squirrel-houses, hutches for rabbits, or bird-cages, than myself: and in the article of cabbage-nets, I had no superior. I even had the hardiness to take in hand the pencil, and studied a whole year the art of drawing. Many figures were the fruit of my labours, which had the merit, at least, of being unparalleled by any production either of art or nature. But before the year was ended, I had occasion to wonder at the progress that may be made, in spite of natural deficiency, by dint alone of practice, for I actually produced three landscapes which a lady thought worthy to be framed and glazed. I then judged it high time to exchange this occupation, lest, by any subsequent productions of inferior merit I should forfeit the honour I had so fortunately acquired.

But gardening was, of all employments, that in which I succeeded best; though even in this I did not suddenly attain perfection.

I began with lettuces and cauliflowers; from them I proceeded to cucumbers; next to melons.

I then purchased an orange tree, to which, in due time I added two or three myrtles. These served me day and night for employment during a whole severe winter. To defend them from the frost, in a situation that exposed them to its severity, cost me much ingenuity, and much attendance.

I contrived to give them a fire heat; and have waded night after night through the snow, with the bellows under my arm, just before going to bed, to give the latest possible puff to the embers, lest the frost should seize them before morning. Very minute beginnings have sometimes important consequences.

From nursing two or three little evergreens, I became

ambitious of a greenhouse, and accordingly built one, which, verse excepted, afforded me amusement for a longer time than any expedient of all the many to which I have fled for refuge from the misery of having nothing to do.

When I left Olney for Weston, I could no longer have a green-house of my own; but in a neighbour's garden I find a better of which the sole management is consigned to me.

I had need take care, when I begin a letter, that the subject with which I set off be of some importance; for before I can exhaust it, be it what it may, I have generally filled my paper. But self is a subject inexhaustible, which is the reason that though I have said little or nothing, I am afraid, worth your hearing, I have only room to add, that I am, my dear Madam, most truly yours,

W. C.

Mrs. Unwin bids me present her best compliments, and say how much she shall be obliged to you for the receipt to make that most excellent cake which came hither in its native pan. There is no production of yours that will not be always most welcome at Weston.

Edward Gibbon meditates farming

October 6, 1771

DEAR HOLROYD, — I sit down to answer your epistle, after taking a very pleasant ride. — A ride! and upon what? — upon a horse.

You lie! — I don't. — I have got a droll little poney, and intend to renew the long-forgotten practice of equitation, as it was known in the world before the second of June of the year of our Lord one thousand seven hundred and sixty-three.

As I used to reason against riding so I can now argue for it; and indeed the principal use I know in human reason is, when called upon, to furnish arguments for what we have an inclination to do.

What do you mean by presuming to affirm that I am of no use here? Farmer Gibbon of no use?

Last week I sold all my hops, and I believe well, at nine guineas a hundred, to a very responsible man.

Some people think I might have got more at Weyhill fair, but that would have been an additional expense, and a great uncertainty.

Our quantity has disappointed us very much; but I think, that besides hops for the family, there will be not less than 500 l.: — no contemptible sum off thirteen small acres, and two of them planted last year only.

This week I let a little farm in Petersfield by auction, and propose raising it from 25 l. to 35 l. *per annum:* — and Farmer Gibbon of no use!

To be serious: I have but one reason for resisting your invitation and my own wishes; that is, I left Mrs. Gibbon alone nearly all last winter, and shall do the same this.

She submits very cheerfully to that state of solitude; but, on sounding her, I am convinced that she would think it unkind were I to leave her at present.

I know you so well, that I am sure you will acquiesce in this reason; and let me make my next visit to Sheffield-Place from town, which I think may be a little before Christmas.

I should like to hear something of the precise time, duration, and extent of your intended tour into Bucks. — Adieu.

The Rev. Laurence Sterne describes his happiness at Coxwould

COXWOULD, *June* 7, 1767

DEAR L——E, — I had not been many days at this peaceful cottage before your letter greeted me with the seal of friendship, and most cordially do I thank you for so kind a proof of your good will — I was truly thankful to hear of the recovery of my sentimental friend — but I would not write to enquire after her, unless I could have sent her the testimony without the tax, for even howd'yes to invalids, or those who have lately been so, either call to mind what is past or what may return — at least I find it so.

I am as happy as a prince at Coxwould — and I wish you could see in how princely a manner I live — 'tis a land of plenty; I sit down alone to venison, fish, wild-fowl or a couple of fowls or ducks, with curds and strawberries and cream, and all the simple plenty which a rich valley (under Hamilton Hills) can produce — with a clean cloth on my table — and a bottle of wine on my right hand to drink your health. I have a hundred hens and chickens about my yard — and not a parishioner catches a hare, or a rabbit, or a trout, but he brings it as an offering to me.

If solitude would cure a love-sick heart, I would give you an invitation — but absence and time lessen no attachment which virtue inspires.

I am in high spirits — care never enters this cottage — I take the air every day in my post-chaise, with two long-tailed horses — they turn out good ones; and as to myself, I think I am better on the whole for the medicines and regimen I submitted in town.

May you, dear, L——, want neither the one nor the other! — Yours truly.

Rural Felicity

Gilbert White on all the finches of the grove

(To Thomas Pennant)

SELBORNE, *September* 2, 1774

DEAR SIR, — Before your letter arrived, and of my own accord, I had been remarking and comparing the tails of the male and female swallow, and this ere any young broods appeared, so that there was no danger of confounding the dames with their *pulli;* and besides, as they were then always in pairs, and busied in the employ of nidification, there could be no room for mistaking the sexes, nor the individuals of different chimneys the one for the other. From all my observations, it constantly appeared that each sex has the long feathers in its tail that give it that forked shape, with this difference, that they are longer in the tail of the male than in that of the female.

Nightingales, when their young first come abroad, and are helpless, make a plaintive and a jarring noise, and also a snapping or cracking, pursuing people along the hedges as they walk: these last sounds seem intended for menace and defiance.

The grasshopper-lark chirps all night in the height of summer.

Swans turn white the second year, and breed the third.

Weasels prey on moles, as appears by their being sometimes caught in mole-traps.

Sparrow-hawks sometimes breed in old crows' nests, and the kestrel in churches and ruins.

There are supposed to be two sorts of eels in the island of Ely. The threads sometimes discovered in eels are their young: the generation of eels is very dark and mysterious.

Hen-harriers breed in the ground, and seem never to settle on trees.

When redstars shake their tails they move them horizontally, as dogs do when they fawn; the tail of a wagtail when in motion bobs up and down like that of a jaded horse.

Hedge-sparrows have a remarkable flirt with their wings in breeding-time; as soon as frosty mornings come they make a very piping plaintive noise.

Many birds which become silent about midsummer reassume their notes again in September, as the thrush, the blackbird, woodlark, willow-wren, etc.; hence August is by much the most mute month the spring, summer, and autumn through. Are birds induced to sing because the temperament of autumn resembles that of spring?

Linnæus ranges plants geographically; palms inhabit the tropics, grasses the temperate zones, and mosses lichens the polar circles; no doubt animals may be classed in the same manner with propriety.

House-sparrows build under the eaves in the spring; as the weather becomes hotter they set out for coolness and rest in plum trees and apple trees. These birds have been known sometimes to build in rooks' nests and sometimes in the forks of boughs under rooks' nests.

As my neighbour was housing a rick, he observed that his dogs devoured all the little red-mice; and his cats ate the common mice, refusing the red.

Red-breasts sing all through the spring, summer and autumn. The reason that they are called autumn songsters is, because in the two first seasons their voices are drowned and lost in the general chorus; in the latter their song becomes distinguishable. Many songsters of the autumn seem to be the young cock red-breasts of that year; notwithstanding the prejudices in their favour, they do much mischief in gardens to the summer fruits.

The titmouse, which early in February begins to make the quaint notes, like the whetting of a saw, is the marsh titmouse: the great titmouse sings with three cheerful joyous notes, and begins about the same time.

Wrens sing all the winter through, frost excepted.

House-martins came remarkably late this year, both in Hampshire and Devonshire: is this circumstance for or against either hiding or migration? Most birds drink sipping at intervals; but pigeons take a long continued draught, like quadrupeds.

Notwithstanding what I have said in a former letter, no grey crows were ever known to breed on Dartmoor; it was my mistake.

The appearance and flying of the *Scarabæus solstitialis*, or fern-chafer, commence with the month of July, and cease about the end of it. These scarabs are the constant food of *Caprimilgi* or fern-owls, through that period. They abound on the chalky downs and in some sandy districts, but not in the clays.

In the garden of the Black Bear Inn in the town of Reading, is a stream or canal running under the stables and out into the fields on the other side of the road; in this water are many carp, which lie rolling about in sight, being fed by travellers, who amuse themselves by tossing them bread; but as soon as the weather grows at all severe, these fishes are no longer seen, because they retire under the stables, where they remain till the return of spring. Do they lie in a torpid state? If they do not, how are they supported?

The note of the white-throat, which is continually repeated, and often attended with odd gesticulation on the wing, is harsh and displeasing. These birds seem of a pugnacious disposition; for they sing with an erected crest and attitudes of rivalry and defiance; are shy and wild in breeding time, avoiding neighbourhoods and haunting lonely lanes and commons; nay, even the very tops of the Sussex downs, where are bushes and coverts; but in July and August they bring their broods into gardens and orchards, and make great havoc among the summer fruits.

The black-cap has in common a full, sweet, deep, loud, and wild pipe; yet that strain is of short continuance, and his motions are desultory; but when that bird sits calmly and engages in song in earnest, he pours forth very sweet but inward melody, and expresses great variety of soft and gentle modulations; superior perhaps to those of any of our warblers, the nightingale excepted.

Black-caps mostly haunt orchards and gardens; while they warble their throats are wonderfully distended.

The song of the redstart is superior, though somewhat like that of the white-throat; some birds have a few more notes than others. Sitting very placidly on the top of a tall tree in a village, the cock sings from morning till night: he affects neighbourhoods, and avoids solitude, and loves to build in orchards and about houses; with us he perches on the vane of a tall may-pole.

The fly-catcher is of all our summer birds the most mute and the most familiar; it also appears the last of any. It builds in a vine, or a sweet briar, against the wall of a house, or in the hole of a wall, or in the end of a beam or plate, and often close to the post of a door where people are going in and out all day long. This bird does not make the least pretension to song, but uses a little inward wailing note when it thinks its young in danger from cats or other annoyances; it breeds but once, and returns early.

Selborne parish alone can and has exhibited at times more than half the birds that are ever seen in all Sweden; the former has produced more than one hundred and twenty species, the latter only two hundred and twenty one. Let me add also that it has shown near half the species that were ever known in Great Britain.

On a retrospect, I observe that my long letter carries with it a quaint and magisterial air, and is very sententious; but when I recollect that you requested stricture and anecdote, I hope you will pardon the didactic manner for the sake of the information it may happen to contain.

Charles James Fox instructs Mr. Gray as to the note of the nightingale

DEAR GRAY, — In defence of my opinion about the nightingales, I find Chaucer, who of all poets seems to have been the fondest of the singing of birds, calls it a *merry* note; and though Theocritus mentions nightingales six or seven times, he never mentions their note as plaintive or melancholy. It is true, he does not call it anywhere merry, as Chaucer does; but by mentioning it with the song of the blackbird, and as answering it, he seems to imply that it was a cheerful note.

Sophocles is against us, but even *he* says, "*lamenting Itys*," and the comparison of her to Electra is rather as to perseverance day and night, than as to sorrow. At all events, a tragic poet is not half so good authority on this question as Theocritus and Chaucer. I cannot light upon the passage in the Odyssey where Penelope's restlessness is compared to the nightingale; but I am sure you will be paid for your hunt, whether you find it or not. The passage in Chaucer is in "Flower and Leaf," page 99. The one I particularly allude to in Theocritus is in his *Epigrams*, I think in the fourth. Dryden has transferred the word *merry* to the gold finch in the "Flower and the Leaf," in deference, may be, to his vulgar error; but pray read his description of the nightingale there: it is quite delightful. I am afraid that I like those researches, as much better than those that relate to Shaftesbury, Sunderland, etc., as I do those better than attending the House of Commons. — Yours affectionately,

C. J. Fox

William Blake and his wife try to lure the Flaxmans to Sussex

HERCULES BUILDINGS, LAMBETH
September 14, 1800

MY DEAREST FRIEND, — I hope you will not think [we] could forget your services to us, or anyway neglect to love and remember with affection even the hem of your garment.

We indeed presume on your kindness in neglecting to have called upon you since my husband's first return from Felpham.

We have been incessantly busy in our great removal; but can never think of going without first paying our proper duty to you and Mr. Flaxman.

We intend to call on Sunday afternoon in Hampstead,

to take farewell; all things being now nearly completed for our setting forth on Tuesday morning.

It is only sixty miles, and Lambeth one hundred, for the terrible desert of London was between.

My husband has been obliged to finish several things necessary to be finished before our migration. The swallows call us, fleeting past our window at this moment.

Oh! how we delight in talking of the pleasure we shall have in preparing you a summer bower at Felpham. And we not only talk, but behold! the angels of our journey have inspired a song to you: —

To my Dear Friend, Mrs. Anna Flaxman

This song to the flower of Flaxman's joy;
To the blossom of hope, for a sweet decoy;
Do all that you can, and all that you may,
To entice him to Felpham and far away.

Away to sweet Felpham, for Heaven is there;
The Ladder of Angels descends through the air;
On the Turret its spiral does softly descend,
Through the village then winds, at my cot it does end.

You stand in the village and look up to Heaven;
The precious stones glitter on flights seventy-seven;
And my brother is there, and my Friend and Thine,
Descend and ascend with the Bread and the Wine.

The Bread of sweet thought and the Wine of delight
Feed the village of Felpham by day and by night;
And at his own door the bless'd hermit does stand,
Dispensing, unceasing, to all the wide land.

W. Blake

Receive my and my husband's love and affection, and believe me to be yours affectionately,

Catherine Blake

VIII

A LICHFIELD CHAPLET

I

(To Mrs. Mompessan)

LICHFIELD, *June* 14, 1791

DID I not manage my mind right stoically, not to touch upon any thing in the shape of an adieu? Was it not, camelion-like, to take the colour of your inclinations, who, I know, love to reserve your embraces for the hour of meeting? Never can I forget how warm those embraces were, when, in the dusk of a vernal evening, I entered your mansion, so embowered and so pleasant, after an absence of almost countless years. Never can I forget the month that glided so swiftly away amid your lovely glades, and in your thrice-dear society. Once more let me thank you for the sweetness and lustre of those recorded days.

As to the sultry morning of our separation, I have not, through life, been so sensible of climatic violence. The white and cloudless concave smote upon us with fiery severity, and clouds of choking dust rose incessantly around us.

But Mrs. Hayley received me with animated gladness,

encompassed with youths of genius — the rising hopes of Derby. They walked with us into Mr. H.'s garden, and returned home with us to supper. Next morning we had levees in succession; half the smart people of that town, interspersed with the militia officers. We past the afternoon and evening at Dr. Darwin's, though he, who unites in himself what Johnson said of James and Garrick, viz. "he who lengthened, and he who gladdened life," the great physician and exquisite poet, was called thirty miles another way, in the exercise of his first power. Mrs. Darwin had an immense party to meet us, for whose apprehended amusement she engaged me, by earnest solicitations, to repeat odes and sonnets. If they were not egregious flatterers, the pleasure the company expressed made it impossible to grudge the exertion, even beneath a sky so torrid.

The next morning we paid some of our visits; and in the evening Mrs. Hayley had more than twenty friends to tea and supper: amongst them a gentleman who, on the instant of his being introduced, impressed my mind with a sentiment in his favour, more passionately tender than I had ever felt for any man on the first interview,

> "Even in the heyday of impetuous youth,
> The spring of life, the bloom of gaudy years."

It was so tender as to force the tears in rivers down my cheeks, during the first half-hour in which he talked to me.

And now, lest your rigid decorum should induce you to censure, without mercy, emotions, at once so rapid and ungovernable, I must whisper to you the age of their inspirer; he is ninety-one — my father's old friend, Mr. Ashby, who preserves, at so late a period, his intellects and sensibility in wonderful power, and with the most attentive politeness; but the sunk mouth of extreme old age, the glazed eye, the hesitating feebleness of accent, the cold clammy hand that pressed mine with affectionate earnestness, all contributed to produce a resemblance to my poor father, so striking as to occasion those emotions I mentioned. He inquired after generations at Lichfield, long passed away, who were his contemporaries, and with whose names my mother had, in childhood, familiarized me, though they had then ceased to exist. He told me that he had often had my mother on his knee, the most beautiful infant of three years old, he said, he ever beheld.

You will imagine how interesting all this to me, who look back upon the years that are fled with all the enthusiasm, though not with the science, of an antiquarian; yet, however interested, gratified, and amused, by the politeness, vivacity, and intelligence of the Derby gentlemen and ladies, I found the heats dreadfully oppressive. Mrs. Hayley's tea-room, and the bedchamber I occupied, are full west. Accustomed to slumber amidst the profoundest silence, and unable, through the sultriness, to shut down my sashes, the street-noises, excessive and incessant, kept me awake two whole nights. I felt the torture of being startled into wakefulness every time the balmy power weighed down my eyelids, and thought of the denunciation against Macbeth. I was never more sensible of its force, and of the misery of being forbid to taste the "chief nourishment at life's feast,"

> "Sleep, that knits up the ravell'd sleeve of care,
> The death of each day's woe, sore labour's bath,
> Balm of hurt minds!"

The stock of health I had acquired in your peaceful village began to vanish fast beneath such fatigue. I sighed for the cool book-room — the hermitage — the shaded lawns and gurgling waters of Woodhouse.

It was with the utmost difficulty that I could retain my purpose of going to Burton, so pressing were the solicitations, on all hands, to prolong my stay in a town whose inhabitants had proved so long pleasant to me — but I did keep my appointment with my friend Mrs. Dalrymple, and arrived at Burton by nine in the evening. Four days passed agreeably away in that visit, except that, during one of them, Mrs. D. was seized with a violent stomach and bowel complaint, but it went off the next day, and I had the satisfaction of leaving her perfectly recovered. It was then that I could jestingly tell her she fell ill on purpose to show off her husband's tender attention, more animated and incessant than I had ever observed in the creation's lords to sick wives. So she sent me home half-inclined to bewail my virginity like Jephtha's daughter.

This good couple long to be acquainted with you, and you would like them. She has intelligence, cheerfulness, and droll humour, in which you so much delight — he has sense, worth, and character, resulting from pleasant oddity and shrewd simplicity of accent and language. You would like him some degrees superadded to your esteem for his good qualities, when you shall know that he lost an estate of 1500l. per annum, by his uncle Colonel Dalrymple's attachment to the fallen house of Stuart, in the year 1745. Mr. and Mrs. D. wish you to pass a day or two with them in some of your journies through Burton, and I wish you would so far oblige and indulge them.

I came home late on Sunday night, and the next morning found the cathedral bowers and lawns in full bloom and beauty, with the addition of four more houses round the area being white-roughcast. It is now completely the milky way, a white zone round the verdant lawn sweetly contrasting the lavish foliage of the scene.

As yet I have seen few of its inhabitants, except dear Lady Gresley and her engaging daughters, and old Mr. Green, to whom I made a point of carrying your good wishes yesterday. That benevolent and industrious collector of antique curiosities breaks fast:

> "His lamp of life is almost spent and done."

Lichfield, or rather the strangers who visit her, will have a great loss if his museum should not survive him, or not be shewn *con amore*, when he shall no longer be found amidst the vestiges of former days. Your kind message cheered his drooping spirits, and he blessed you with moist eyes.

You remember my observing to you how much our language had become, even in common conversation, Latinized, since Dr. Johnson's writings were familiar to people, and since his fine style had been so generally adopted by ingenious writers. I heard some ladies at Burton, who neither have, nor pretend to, bookish knowledge, use the following words with prompt spontaneity in conversing on common topics, viz. "literature, literary, hilarity, stipulate, excruciating, delusive, juvenile, temerity, contemporary, phenomenon, popular, conservatory," etc. etc. Twenty years ago, scarce one of those words would have been understood, much less used by the generality of private gentlewomen. I like this growing Latinity — it rids us of a number of those hissing *s's* that deform our language, which becomes more harmonious and full for their dismission. Adieu, my dear friend!

II

(To Mrs. Adey)

Buxton, *June* 14, 1793

I AM invoking the Naiads of these warm soft springs, to wash away the dregs of that obscure and long disease, which, assuming various forms, has oppressed me since the birth-day of this year. There was reason to hope, that bathing and drinking the waters would have been of great use; but, lo! a violent cold now shivers through my veins. The weather is perverse. After a long drought, and cloudless horizon, no sooner came luckless I, than loud and keen blew the north, and rainy clouds drew their dark trains over the mountains. If this hoarse soreness on my lungs should settle into one of my fierce hereditary coughs, the prospect of the north coast will vanish from my purposes, and I shall shrink back home to quiet and domestic nursing.

Though, as yet, the young gay crowds do not swarm through our golden Crescent, hitherto have my hours passed pleasantly in musical parties, and in little conversations of intelligence and interest. I am under the same roof with amiable and lovely Mrs. Sedley, and dear Mrs. Greaves, of our little city. Except the latter, I did not, on my first arrival, personally know a single being of those various groups that inhabit the Crescent, or resort to it in preference to the less splendid dwellings of olden time. My next favourite after sweet Mrs. Sedley, among these stranger tribes, is Lady Clerk, from the environs of Edinburgh. She is here with her laughter-loving husband, who very shrewdly knows life and manners, and the rudiments of many sciences; who plays slow Scotch airs on the violin with the skill of a professor, and the pathos of a lover. Sir John Clerk seems to idolize his lady, who is still very handsome, though no longer a girl. Her figure verges to *en bon point;* but her step, her air, her address, are spirited and graceful; and her conversation is frank, interesting, and gay. Her apartments attract the ingenious and polite of both sexes; and if her parties are not large, they are select.

And Miss Delabere, the engaging sister of my beloved Mrs. Granville, I was delighted to find here. Though personally strangers, we knew much of each other. Fast-fading health was the motive of her journey. The paleness of her cheek, the languor of her step, are rendered pleasing by that pensive sweetness of smile, that touching softness of voice, which are often more conciliating than even the warm glow of independent health, and render even defect lovely.

Sir John E——'s daughters were, on my first arrival, the belles of the scene. The eldest is strikingly handsome, with an air of dignity and fashion, and, as she passes, irresistibly attracts the eye. I had no acquaintance with these nymphs, nor desired it. They have an assured and repulsive haughtiness of look and step, which, though not incompatible with grace, destroys all its interest. —

"The toss of quality, and high-bred fleer."

They soon left us; and to their claim of handsomest, amid a dearth of beauty, succeeded the two Miss C——s, accompanying their portly, handsome, though gouty, father; a very shy country gentleman, who says little, and has but one theme, viz. the hereditary powers and beauties of horn-cattle. His second daughter is most admired; tall and well-shaped; a brunette complexion, of high bloom; dark large round eyes; the full lips and aquiline nose of the Cæsarian medals. Her sister has the same features, upon a less scale; but has neither the height nor bloom of the younger, who possesses a most uncommon talent for mechanics. She builds little coaches, chaises, and phaetons, which are said to be perfect models; and has no assistance in making the wheels, the windows, or any other part. These young ladies are unaffected; but neither in their persons, their countenance, or manner, is there an atom of grace or expression; and they extremely want that obliging vivacity, which is at once so natural and so lovely in youth.

When I left home, Mrs. Cobb was in somewhat better health, and her intellects clearer than they had been some time. Miss Adey is in robust vigour of frame, and has every prospect of longevity; but there is no rational dependence upon these vital perspectives.

This is my native country, and I gaze, with thrills of filial tenderness, even on these wild and barren hills. Tell your beloved Mr. Adey, that I purpose going next week to Eyam, the village of my birth, the home of my early infancy; and whither I often used to accompany my father on his summer residences there. I cannot resist the desire of indulging this mournful luxury, in a scene which bears such striking traces of the dear and for ever lost. There is more scenic beauty and cultivated umbrage round Eyam than amidst those naked and monotonous mountains.

Mr. Adey's affectionate heart feels the force of local impressions on every seldom visit to his native Lichfield, and will sympathize with me in the sensations that induce this little excursion.

I congratulate you on the public virtue of your favourite friend, Mr. Windham. His talents have been long distinguished; and he has now proved his patriotism sincere, by preferring the welfare of his country to private friendship and party influence. Adieu!

III

(To Mrs. Mompessan)

BRIDLINGTON QUAY, YORKSHIRE
August 15, 1793

THAT you have been so ill, dear friend, I am sorry, but comforted that, writing in a state of convalescence, your disease is amongst the number of past evils, for which concern rises in our bosom, "shorn of its stings."

This long excursion has afforded me many pleasures, besides having, as I hope, contributed to the restoration of my health. At Buxton, I formed a friendship with excellent Mrs. Sedley, which the resistless disappointer of human wishes has most unexpectedly nipt in its first interesting expansion. — On my road to the North coast, after travelling through long tracks of brown and thistly sterility, scenes of the highest and most ornamented cultivation rose to my eye, on the banks of the majestic Humber, which is there several miles broad; and it seemed a drive of several miles through a gay garden, the pleasure-grounds of each elegant and thick-sown villa extending from one to another. I dined with my dear and old friend Mrs. Collins, whose virtues glow, and whose intellectual lights burn brightly as your own, in despite of the snows which time has shed upon your mutual foreheads.

In the evening, I proceeded where, four miles farther, the known woods and lawns of Westella, haunts of my youth, adorn the banks of that flood of liquid silver, which rolls in their view. I was received with animated and cordial welcome; its glow seemed proportioned to the length of our separation. My valued friends were become venerable, with the children of those sons playing round their knees, who were themselves scarce more than children on my last visit to that dear scene. It is on returning to a place, after a very long absence, that we scarcely credit our eyes, when they show us a new generation rising in up the interim. The intervening space is annihilated, by the strong impression we retain of the living objects we had left there, and by the sameness of the local ones.

I found good and generous Mrs. Sykes slowly recovering from a dangerous and long illness, and her engaging and accomplished daughter feeble and languid, by the long pressure of filial anxieties and exertions, upon a very delicate constitution. They obligingly offered to accompany me to Bridlington, but were too unwell to encounter the company and hurries of Scarborough. My promise to Mr. Dewes interfering, we agreed, that if he and his party left that coast before my aqueous discipline was performed, as to duration, I should complete it on this less splendid shore, where they agreed to meet me. . . .

Hither I came on the 5th instant, Mr. and Mrs. Sykes

having arrived a few hours before me. Two agreeable young ladies of their intimacy, Miss Horners of Hull, joined us the ensuing day. Thus are we a party of five in the same lodgings, and on the edge of the vast German Ocean; we inhale its saline gales, and hope they will be salubrious. As yet I have only been able to bathe twice, so angrily turbulent have I found *ma mère*. A boarded pier, one hundred and twenty yards in length, and on which nine people may walk abreast, juts out into her bosom, not fifty paces from us, and balances all the other superiorities of Scarborough. The sea-sands are always either too wet or too heavy for comfortable walking — but this pier forms an admirable public walk. There all the company of the place resort, — and there the ocean gales rise on all sides around us, freely as we could taste them in a boat. Here we walk or sit, very often in the day, frequently when the huge billows are raging and lashing the pier on every side.

Several families of consequence are at this place, with whom, being known to Mrs. Sykes, we exchange morning visits. In the evenings I generally read aloud, while the rest work.

Pretty Mrs. John Gisbon is of the number, with her boyish-looking, but highly intelligent husband. They were so good to take me yesterday in their coach an airing on the edges of the cliffs. — The finest and mildest sun shed his brilliants in the mighty waters, on which all the winds lay asleep. When the horses turned homewards, we descended to the sands, and observed the pretty grey and white seagulls taking their noon-meal of shrimps on the edges of the waves, that but just purled up the shore. The vast sea was of a bright blueish-green, verifying Ossian's description, when he says, "the blue waves of Ullin rolled in light."

But, O! the delusive smiles of that capricious element! In the afternoon, the wind rising and blowing east, the billows began to chafe and foam. Their rage increased as the evening came on, and then it was that "the waters grew dark as they rose." It was the spring-tides, and they surged to the shore with a prodigious and turbulent flood.

Mr. Daniel Sykes joined our party, since I began this letter some days ago, by engagements prevented from finishing it sooner. This young gentleman and myself have not met since his school-days. In the beauty of his face, and the polish of his address, he rises, to my observation, the flower of the Westella house. All its sons have merit, one of them has genius and wit, but he only has the graces; nor exist they alone, or with a frivolous mind, but are the fascinating ornaments of distinguished talents and generous worth.

So the bloody Marat is fallen by female heroism, and the Generals Custine and Miranda are condemned, with the legislator Brissot! Thus it is, that the godless and lawless republic, like Sin, makes the wages of his servants death. Adieu.

IV

(To David Somervell, Esq.)

LICHFIELD, *March* 17, 1795

IT flatters me that you like my little poem on Hoyle lake. I have really not exaggerated the mild *agrémens* of the scene. The handsome hotel, built since you saw it, the little appendant white cottages, scattered around, to supply it with milk, butter, etc., diffuse an air of cheerful and social comfort, where you saw only barren and lonely downs. The rich and varied scenery on the Flintshire coast, rising from the waters of the Dee, form, when the azure mirror is full, a soft and marine landscape, recompensing the beautiful absence of rocky grandeur, and the terrific grace of oceanic sublimity.

Your account of the Shakespearean discovery is very interesting — but my faith is not implicit. The absence of the indecent passages in the copy of Lear, looks suspicious. Obscene wit occurs so often in his other plays, and in Lear it is of such biting shrewdness, that, however responsible in inclination the performer might be to foist in passages of that nature, the infinite satiric wit of those which are scattered through that play, proclaim their genuine descent, "trumpet-tongued."

The internal evidence which the Vortigern must supply, either for or against the originality of these productions, will, in time, by the accumulating suffrages of those who are competent to judge and decide upon poetic claims, either sink them in oblivion, or gather them to the treasures left us by that great master.

If the business should be surreptitious; he is a bold man who attempts to shoot in the strong bow of our own Ulysses. I believe there is one, and only one existing, who has the power of exciting doubt, if not faith, in the discriminating, by an effort so arduous.

That man is Jephson. His bold and figurative style in Narbon, and in the Law of Lombardy, resembles Shakespeare extremely: — not servilely, but with freedom, strength, and happiness. The little notice which has been taken of those plays, compared with their true claims to distinction, convince me that if Shakespeare had lived and written in these days, his fame and himself had not been contemporaries.

With your censure of a line in that fine ode of Gray's, on the installation of the Duke of Grafton at Cambridge, I do not quite accord. In this the concluding stanza —

> "Through the wild waves, as they roar,
> With watchful eye, and dauntless mien,
> Thy steady cause of honour keep;
> Nor fear the rocks nor dread the shore,
> The star of Brunswick smiles serene
> And gilds the horrors of the deep."

You say that, without an effort of memory, you never could recollect the second line of that stanza, and have at length discovered that it is the author's fault, being a superfluous line, and the sense of the passage complete without it. I confess the sense of the passage complete without that parenthetic line, but it appears to me of vital essentiality to the picture. Excluding it, there remains, it is true, a clear allusion to an able mariner combating maritime dangers, but no distinct image. In that second line, the magic of the poetic wand instantly transforms the minister of state into the skilful and intrepid naval commander, standing firm on the deck, and eluding, "with watchful eye, and dauntless mien," the fury of the tempest: while it changes our monarch into the polar-star, discovering the rocks, and shining a way in the sea, and a path in the mighty waters. There is happy, and I think Horatian spirit, in your ode written on the northern cruise. The address to the moon is beautiful, — particularly in the manner of Horace.

Mischiefs, many and various, descend upon our Island — a relentless winter, with its long frosts and resistless floods, has augmented the miseries of a rash and ill-managed war, and almost destroyed the verisimilitude of one feature in Johnson's beautiful picture of our unhappy country, the blessings of which seem to transcend the faith of his Greenlander: "We live not, my fair, in those fabled countries which your stanzas so wantonly describe, where the whole year is divided into short days and nights; where its inhabitants may pass from one extremity of the land to another, through ways inclosed with trees, and over walls raised upon the inland waters."

Our young prince comes to us at an inauspicious period. Since her royal lover so long declined the hymeneal chain, he had better have waited till the lilies and olives of peace might enwreath it. O! that our rulers would endeavour to procure them for the insignia of British sway, rather than those ensanguined laurels, which, now so evidently placed beyond its reach — stamp the continuation of this desperate struggle to obtain them, with very criminal rashness, and with folly that amounts to infatuation. It is time, it has long been time, to take care of our existence as an independent nation. As for the enslaving, the tyrannous, the murderous, the blasphemous anarchists — Vengeance is mine, saith the Lord, and I will repay it.

How stood your health the seldom-paralleled severity of last winter? the long frost and its undulating dissolution?

> "What art thou, frost? and whence are thy keen stores
> Derived, thou secret, all-invading power,
> Which e'en th' illusive flood cannot fly?"

Do you admire the charming poet who asks that question in his Seasons? — Thomson! great painter of nature, this art of all hours.

Dropping eyelids reproach my pen for having invaded the hours of rest. It stands corrected, and bids you farewell!

IX

OUR VILLAGE RECEIVES THE NEWS

I

(B. R. Haydon to Miss Mitford)

EDINBURGH, *December* 5, 1820

I DINED with Walter Scott, and was delighted with the unaffected simplicity of his family. Jeffrey has a singular expression, poignant, bitter, piercing — as if his countenance never lighted up but at the perception of some weakness in human nature. Whatever you praise to Jeffrey, he directly chuckles out some error that you did not perceive. Whatever you praise to Scott, he joins heartily with yourself, and directs your attention to some additional beauty. Scott throws a light on life by the beaming geniality of his soul, and so dazzles you that you have no time or perception for anything but its beauties: while Jeffrey seems to revel in holding up his hand before the light in order that he may spy out its deformities. The face of Scott is the expression of a man whose great pleasure has been to shake nature by the hand, while to point at her with his finger has certainly, from the expression of his face, been the chief enjoyment of Jeffrey. . . .

Wilson I think the most powerful mind I have yet encountered here. He is a man of great genius, and will be a distinguished figure. No allusion has ever passed about the "Magazine." They have treated me with great respect, and it would be beneath me to think of what is passed. There is a great concentration of talent in Edinburgh, but yet they have one peculiarity of a small town. Their stories at table derive their relish from their individuality. They all relate to some one local celebrity that you must know in order to enjoy the story. In London, on the contrary, the stories always refer to some general principle of human character that is found in all the world. But here, they are about "Davie," or "Dick," or "Sandy," or some one you never heard of, who is either lame or stutters, or squints, or has some defect, which is not general, but personal and peculiar. This, I suppose, must always be the case where the population is limited, and society confined to a small space.

II

September 8, 1822

POOR Hazlitt! He who makes so free with the follies of his friends, is of all mortals the most open to ridicule. To hear him repeat in a solemn tone and with agitated mouth the things of love he said to her (to convince you that he made love in the true gallant way), to feel the beauty of the sentiment, and then look up and see his old hard, weather-beaten, saturnine, metaphysical face — the very antidote of the sentiment — twitching all sorts of ways, is really enough to provoke a saint to laughter. He has a notion that women have never liked him. Since this affair he has dressed in the fashion, and keeps insinuating his improved appearance. *He springs up to show you his pantaloons!* What a being it is! His conversation is now a mixture of disappointed revenge, passionate remembrances, fiendish hopes, and melting lamentations. I feel convinced his metaphysical habits of thinking have rendered him insensible to moral duty, etc.

III

September 1823

OH, human nature! and human criticism! Did mankind know the motives which instigate all criticism on living talent, or within ten years after its existence, how cautious it would be of suffering itself to be led by modern critics! . . .

When Keats was living, I could not get Hazlitt to admit Keats had common talents. Death seems to cut off all apprehensions that our self-love will be wounded by acknowledging genius. But let us see, and sift the motives of this sudden change. "Blackwood's" people Hazlitt would murder, morally or physically, no matter which, but to murder them he wishes. To suppose Keats's death *entirely* brought on by "Blackwood's" attacks is too valuable and mortal a blow to be given up. With the wary cunning of a thoroughbred modern review writer, he dwells on this touching subject, so likely to be echoed by all who have suffered by "Blackwood's" vindictive animosities. *Now*, Keats is an immortal; before, he was a pretender! *Now*, his sensitive mind withered under their "murderous criticism," when, had Keats been a little more prominent, Hazlitt, as soon as any man, would have given him the first stab! He thus revenges his own mortification by pushing forward the shattered ghost of poor fated Keats.

Hazlitt and his innamorata have now gone to Italy, the land of Art, and he has left the "land of spinning-jennies and Sunday schools," as he says — and, as he forgot to say, the land also of Shakespeare and Milton, Bacon and Newton, Hampden and Locke.

IV

May 31, 1824

I HAVE not yet read Byron's "Conversations," but there was an anecdote in one of the extracts which confirms what I heard long since, but which I could not depend on before. He had an aversion to see women *eat*. Colonel —— was at Byron's house in Piccadilly. Lady Byron in the room, and "luncheon" was brought in — veal cutlets, etc. She began eating. Byron turned round in disgust and said, "Gormandizing beast!" and taking up the tray, threw the whole luncheon into the hall. Lady Byron cried, and left the room.

Byron hated to be interrupted when he was writing, then why she did interrupt him? Because *she* thought it was a whim. To her and her dear delightful maid it might appear a whim; but if, at that moment, he was conceiving some beautiful thoughts, what can you think of a woman who, for some trifle, would interrupt her husband's conceptions? I have never said a cold thing, much more a harsh one, to Mary, but if she had come into my room and asked me if I would like roast mutton for dinner when I was conceiving "Lazarus," I think she would never have come in a second time. Setting aside that, women of rank and family are not fitted for "Love and Genius." Their pride, their importance, their habits of separate rooms, footmen, carriages, maids, and confidantes, are inconsistent with the care a man of genius requires. But every wind blows intelligence that we are right in our estimation of Byron's character.

V

May 31, 1824

A FRIEND of mine has been spending some time at Sir Walter Scott's. Scott is liable to great intrusions of every kind. A stupid chattering fellow got at him by a letter, and stayed a week. He was a great bore, and my friend and another visitor were obliged one day to retire to a window to avoid laughing outright. Sir Walter hobbled up to them and said, "Come, come, young gentlemen, be more respectful. I assure you it requires no small talents to be a *decided bore!*" I like this! there is the geniality of the "Unknown" in it.

VI

August 18, 1826

THE other night I paid my butcher; one of the miracles of these times, you will say. Let me tell you, I have all my life been seeking for a butcher whose respect for genius predominated over his love of gain. I could not make out, before I dealt with this man, his excessive desire that I should be his customer; his sly hints as I passed his shop that he had "a bit of South Down very fine; a sweetbread, perfection; and a calf's foot that was all jelly without bone!" The other day he called, and I had him sent up into the painting-room. I found him in great admiration of "Alexander." "Quite alive, sir!" "I am glad you think so," said I. "Yes, sir; but, as I have often said to my sister, you could not have painted that picture, sir, if you had not eat my meat, sir!" "Very true, Mr. Sowerby." "Ah! sir, I have a fancy for *genus*, sir!" "Have you, Mr. Sowerby?" "Yes, sir; Mrs. Siddons, sir, has eat my meat, sir; never was *such a woman for chops, sir!*" — and he drew up his beefy, shiny face, clean shaved, with a clean blue cravat under his chin, a clean jacket, a clean apron, and a pair of hands that would pin an ox to the earth if he was obstreperous — "Ah! sir, she was a wonderful crayture!" "She was, Mr. Sowerby." "Ah! sir, when she used to act that there character, you see (but Lord, such a head! as I say to my sister) — that there woman, sir, that murders a king between 'em!" "Oh! Lady Macbeth." "Ah, sir, that's it — Lady Macbeth — I used to get up with the butler behind her carriage when she acted, and, as I used to see her looking quite wild, and all the people quite frightened, 'Ah, ha! my lady,' says I, 'if it wasn't for my meat, though, you wouldn't be able to do *that!*'" "Mr. Sowerby, you seem to be a man of feeling; will you take a glass of wine?" After a bow or two, down he sat, and by degrees his heart opened. "You see, sir, I have fed Mrs. Siddons, sir; John Kemble, sir; Charles Kemble, sir; Stephen Kemble, sir; and Madame Catalini, sir; Morland the painter, and I beg your pardon, sir, and *you*, sir." "Mr. Sowerby, you do me honour." "Madame Catalini, sir, was a wonderful woman for sweetbreads; but the Kemble family, sir, the gentlemen, sir, rump-steaks and kidneys in general was their taste; but Mrs. Siddons, sir, she liked chops, sir, as much as you do, sir," etc. etc. I soon perceived that the man's ambition was to feed genius. I shall recommend you to him; but is he not a capital fellow? But a little acting with his remarks would make you roar with laughter. Think of Lady Macbeth eating chops! Is this not a peep behind the curtain? I remember Wilkie saying that at a public dinner he was looking out for some celebrated man, when at last he caught a glimpse for the first time of a man whose books he had read with care for years, picking the leg of a roast goose, perfectly abstracted!

X

THE LADY OF LES ROCHERS

(Translated by Janet Aldis)

I

Madame de Sévigné to her daughter

PARIS, *December* 15, 1670

I AM going to tell you of an event which is the most astonishing, the most surprising, the most marvellous, the most miraculous, the most magnificent, the most bewildering, the most unheard-off, the most singular, the most extraordinary, the most incredible, the most unexpected, the greatest, the least, the most rare, the most common, the most public, the most private till to-day, the most brilliant, the most enviable, in short, an event to which there is only one parallel to be found in past ages, and even that not an exact one; an event which we cannot believe in Paris (how then can it be believed in Lyons?), an event which makes everybody exclaim, "Lord, have mercy upon us!" an event which causes the greatest joy to Madame de Rohan and Madame d'Hauterive; an event, in fact, which will take place on Sunday next, when those who are present will doubt the evidence of their senses; an event which, though it is to happen on Sunday, may perhaps not be accomplished on Monday. I cannot persuade myself to tell you. Guess what it is! I give you three guesses. Do you give it up? Well, then, I must tell you. Monsieur de Lauzun is to be married next Sunday at the Louvre — guess to whom! I give you four guesses, I give you ten, I give you a hundred. Madame de Coulanges says, "It is not very difficult to guess, it is Madame de la Vallière." You are quite wrong, Madame. "It is Mademoiselle de Retz, then." No, it is not; you are very provincial.

"Dear me, how stupid we are," you exclaim, "it is Mademoiselle de Colbert, of course." You are farther off than ever. "Then it must be Mademoiselle de Créqui." You are no nearer. Well, I find I must tell you. He is to marry on Sunday at the Louvre, with the King's permission, Mademoiselle, Mademoiselle de — Mademoiselle — guess the name! he is to marry Mademoiselle, my faith! by my faith! my sworn faith! Mademoiselle, La Grande Mademoiselle; Mademoiselle, daughter of the late Monsieur; Mademoiselle, granddaughter of Henry IV; Mademoiselle d'Eu, Mademoiselle de Dombes, Mademoiselle de Montpensier, Mademoiselle d'Orléans; Mademoiselle, first cousin to the King; Mademoiselle, once destined for the throne; Mademoiselle, the only person in France worthy of Monsieur. Here is a fine subject for conversation. If you cry out, if you are beside yourselves, if you say we are deceiving you, that it is false, that we are laughing at you, that it is a pretty joke, that it is a very poor invention; if, in fact, you abuse us, we shall say you are right, for we have done the same ourselves. Adieu. You will see by the letters you receive by this post whether I am telling you the truth or not.

II

At M. de La Rochefoucauld's House
Friday evening, April 24, 1671

HERE, then, I make up my packet. I had intended to tell you that the King arrived yesterday evening at Chantilly; and that he hunted a stag by moonlight. The illuminations were wonderful; the fireworks were a little eclipsed by our friend the moon, it is true, but the evening, the supper, and the entertainment, all went off admirably. . . . But what do you think I learned when I came here? I am not yet recovered, and hardly know what I write. Vatel, the great Vatel, late *maître d'hotel* to M. Foucquet, and now acting in that capacity to M. Le Prince, that man of such distinguished capability above all others, whose abilities were equal to governing a State; this man whom I knew so well, finding that the fish did not come, ran himself through with a sword. . . .

I wrote to you last Friday that he had stabbed himself, and here are the particulars of the affair. The King arrived there on Thursday evening, and the hunt, the illuminations, the moonlight, the promenade, the banquet in a place strewn with jonquils, were all that could be desired. Supper was served, but there were some tables at which there was no roast meat, because Vatel had had to provide several dinners that had not been expected. This greatly troubled Vatel, who was heard to say several times, "I have lost my honour; I cannot endure this disgrace!"

"My head is quite bewildered," he said to Gourville; "I have not slept for twelve nights; I wish you would help me to give orders."

Gourville did all he could to assist and console him, but the failure of the roast meat — which, however, did not happen at the King's table, but at some of the other twenty-five — was always in his mind. Gourville mentioned it to the Prince, who went to Vatel's room, and said to him —

"Everything is admirably managed, Vatel; nothing could be better than the King's supper."

"Your goodness overwhelms me, Monseigneur," replied Vatel, "but I know there was no roast meat at two tables."

"Not at all," said the Prince; "do not distress yourself, and all will be well. . . ."

At four o'clock the next morning, Vatel went round and found every one asleep. He met one of the under-purveyors, who had just brought in a load of fish.

"Is this all?" asked Vatel.

"Yes, sir," said the man, who did not know that Vatel had ordered fish from all the seaports round.

He waited for some time, but the other purveyors did not come; his head grew distracted; he believed there was no more fish to be had. He then went to Gourville and exclaimed —

"Sir, I cannot outlive this disgrace; I shall lose my honour and reputation;" but Gourville only laughed at him.

Vatel, however, went to his room, and, placing the hilt of his sword against the door, after two ineffectual attempts succeeded the third time in forcing the sword through his heart, and he fell dead.

At that instant the purveyors arrived with the fish, and search was made for Vatel, to distribute it. They went to his room; they knocked, and receiving no answer, they broke open the door, and discovered him lying in a pool of blood. . . .

III

LES ROCHERS, *June* 28, 1671

WE read Tasso with pleasure, and I am fairly proficient in the language, thanks to the excellent masters I have had. My son makes La Mousse read *Cléopatre*, and I listen to him whether I will or not, and am amused. My son is going to Lorraine; we shall be very dull in his absence. You know how it vexes me to see the breaking up of an agreeable party, and how delighted I am when I see a carriage driving off with people who have wearied me to death all day; upon which we might make the observation that bad company is more desirable than good. I recollect all the odd things we used to say when you were here, and all you said yourself, and all you did; the thought of you never leaves me; and then, again, I suddenly remember where you are, my imagination represents to me an immense space and a great distance; suddenly your Castle bounds the prospect, and I am displeased at the walls that enclose your mall. Ours is surprisingly beautiful, and the young nursery is delightful. I take pleasure in rearing their little heads to the clouds; and frequently, without considering consequences or my own interests, cut down the tall trees because their shade is bad for my young ones. My son looks on at all these proceedings, but I do not allow him to interfere.

Pilois continues to be a great favourite with me, and I prefer his conversation to that of many who have the title of chevalier in the Parlement of Rennes. I have grown rather more unceremonious than you, for the other day I let a carriageful of the Fouesnel family go home through a tremendous rain for want of a little pressing them with a good grace to stay; but I could not get the compliment to pass my lips! . . . I have just been writing to Vivonne about a captain of a group of gypsies, whose confinement I have begged him to make as easy as possible, without detriment to the King's service. You must know that among the band of Bohemians I mentioned to you the other day, was a young girl who danced extremely well, and who put me very much in mind of you. I was pleased with her, and she begged me to write to Provence in favour of her grandfather. "Where is he?" I asked. "He is at Marseilles," said she, with as much composure and unconcern as if she had said, "He is at Vincennes." He was a man of singular merit, it appears, in his way: in short, I promised to write about him. I immediately thought of Vivonne, and I send you the letter I have written to him. If you are not on such terms with him as will allow me to jest, you may burn it; but if you are friendly with his corpulency, and my letter will save you the trouble of writing one, seal it and send it to him. I could not refuse this request to the poor girl, and to the best-danced minuet that I have seen since the days of Mademoiselle de Sévigné. She had just your air; with good teeth and fine eyes, and was about your height.

IV

I have bought some stuff like your last petticoat to make a morning-gown, and it is very beautiful. There is a shade of green in it, but violet predominates; in short, I could not resist the purchase. They would have me line it with flame-colour, but this appeared to me inconsistent; for while the outside is expressive of frailty, the inside would have signified impenitence, even obduracy, so I fixed on a white taffety. I have put myself to very little expense, as I hate Brittany, and shall be most economical till I come to Provence, that I may then support the position and dignity of the middle-aged wonder that you have represented me to be.

V

AUX ROCHERS, *November* 13, 1675

. . . YOU are surprised to hear I have a little dog; this is how it happened. One day I was calling a little dog which belongs to a lady who lives at the end of the park. Madame de Tarente said to me: "What! do you like dogs? I will send you one of the prettiest you have ever seen." I thanked her, and said I had made a resolution never again to indulge myself in an affection of that kind; so the subject was dropped, and I thought no more of it. A few days after, I saw a footman bringing a little dog-kennel, all decorated with ribbons, and out of this pretty kennel jumped a little perfumed dog, quite extraordinary beautiful, with ears, coat, and sweet breath like a little sylph, the fairest of the fair. I was never more surprised or more embarrassed.

I would have returned it, but the servant would not take it back; though the chamber-maid who had reared it was fit to die with grief for the loss of it. It is Marie who is so fond of it; he sleeps in his kennel in Beaulieu's room, and eats nothing but bread. I try not to become too attached to it, but it begins to like me, and I am afraid I shall succumb to its affection. This is the story which I beg you not to tell to Marphise (her pet dog) at Paris, for I dread her reproaches. But it is the cleanliest little animal you ever saw; its name is Fidèle, a name, I believe, that the lovers of the Princess have never deserved, though they have been of some importance. Some day I will amuse you with her adventures. Her style, it is true, is full of faintings, and I do not think she has had sufficient leisure to love her daughter, not at least as I love mine. More than one heart would be necessary to love so many things at once, and I perceive every day that the great fish eat up all the little ones. If you are, as you say, very preservative, I am very much obliged to you. I cannot too highly prize the love I have for you. I do not know from what dangers it has guarded me, but if it were from fire or from water, it could not be dearer to me than it is.

VI

WEDNESDAY, *May* 20, 1676

TO-DAY I began the pump operation, and it is not a bad foretaste of purgatory. The patient is quite naked in a little underground room, where there is a tube of hot water which a woman directs wherever you wish. Behind the curtain is a person who sustains your courage for half an hour. A physician of Ganot fell to my lot; a very worthy man, who is neither a quack nor a bigot; I shall keep him though it cost me my cap, for the doctors here are unbearable, and this man amuses me; he has wit and honesty, and knows the world. He talked to me the whole time I was under torture. Just think of a spout of water pouring over one or other of your poor limbs! It is first applied to every part of the body to rouse the spirits, and then to the affected joints; but when it comes to the nape of the neck, the heat produces such a surprise that it is impossible to describe it. However, it is necessary to suffer, and we do suffer, but we are not quite scalded to death; and we are then put into a warm bed, where we perspire profusedly, and in this way we are cured.

It is like taking a new lease of life and health, and if I could only see and embrace you once more, with a heart overflowing with tenderness and joy, you would perhaps again call me your *bellissima madre*, and I should not give up the title of *mère-beauté* with which M. de Coulanges has honoured me.

Madame de Brissac was ill to-day, and remained in bed, with her hair dressed so beautifully, and looking so handsome, that she was fit to turn everybody's head. I wished you could have seen how prettily she managed her sufferings, her eyes, her arms, and her cries, with her hands lying helplessly in the quilt, and looking for the sympathy she expected from all bystanders. I was quite overcome with tenderness and admiration as I watched this little performance, and though it is so excellent that my evident attention must have given much satisfaction. Just think this scene was played entirely on account of the Abbé Bayard, Saint Hérem, Montjeu and Plancy! My child, when I remember with what simplicity you are ill, and the calmness in your pretty face, you seem to me a mere bungler! What a difference! I found it very amusing.

VII

I love Pauline; you describe her as pretty and good-humoured; I can see her running everywhere and telling every one of the taking of Philipsburg. Love, love your daughter, my dear child; it is the most natural and delightful occupation in the world.

XI

CARLYLE DISCOVERS LONDON

Thomas Carlyle to Alexander Carlyle

I

June 25, 1824

. . . WHEN I see you I will tell you of Westminster Abbey; and St. Paul's, the only edifice that ever struck me with a proper sense of grandeur. I was hurrying along Cheapside into Newgate Street among a thousand bustling pigmies and the innumerable jinglings and rollings and crashings of many-coloured Labour, when all at once in passing from the abode of John Gilpin, stunned by the tumult of his restless compeers, I looked up from the boiling throng through a little opening at the corner of the street — and there stood St. Paul's — with its columns and friezes, and massy wings of bleached yet unworn stone; with its statues and its graves around it; with its solemn dome four hundred feet above me, and its gilded ball and cross gleaming in the evening sun, piercing up into the heaven through the vapours of our earthly home! It was silent as Tadmor of the Wilderness; gigantic, beautiful, enduring; it seemed to frown with a rebuking pity on the vain scramble which it overlooked: at its feet were tombstones, above it was the everlasting sky, within priests perhaps were chanting hymns; it seemed to transmit with a stern voice the sounds of Death, Judgment and Eternity through all the frivolous and fluctuating city. I saw it oft and from various points, and never without new admiration.

. . . .

Did you get *Meister*, and how do you *dis*like it? For really it is a most mixed performance, and though intellectually good, much of it is morally bad. It is making way here perhaps — but slowly: a second edition seems a dubious matter. No difference! I have the produce of the first lying here beside me in hard notes of the Bank of England, and fear no weather. I bought myself a suit of fine clothes for six pounds; a good watch for six; and these were nearly all my purchases. . . .

II

December 14, 1824

MY DEAR ALICK, — . . . Your letter found me in due season; and a welcome visitant it was. I had got the *Courier* that preceded it, and the intelligence of your proceedings and welfare was no small relief to me. You must thank our Mother in my name in the warmest terms for her kind note, which I have read again and again with an attention rarely given to more polished compositions. The sight of her rough true-hearted writing is more to me than the finest penmanship and the choicest rhetoric. It takes me home to honest kindness, and affection that will never fail me. You also

I must thank for your graphic picture of Mainhill and its neighbourhood. How many changes happen in this restless roundabout of life within a little space! . . .

In London, or rather in my own small sphere of it, there has nothing sinister occurred since I wrote last. After abundant scolding, which sometimes rose to the very borders of bullying, those unhappy people [the publishers] are proceeding pretty regularly with *the* Book; a fifth part of it is already printed; they are also getting a portrait of *Schiller* engraved for it; and I hope in about six weeks the thing will be off my hands. It will make a reasonable looking book; somewhat larger than a volume of *Meister*, and done in somewhat of the same style. In the course of printing I have various matters to attend to; proofs to read; additions, alterations to make; which furnishes me with a very *canny* occupation for the portion of the day I can devote to labour. I work some three or four hours; read for amusement chiefly about as long; walk about these dingy streets, and talk with originals for the rest of the day. On the whole I have not been happier for many a long month: I feel content to let things take their turn till I am free of engagements; and then — for a stern and serious *tuffle* with my Fate, which I have vowed and determined to alter from the very bottom, health and all! This *will not* be impossible, or even I think extremely difficult. Far beyond a million of "weaker vessels," than I are sailing very comfortably along the tide of life just here. What good is it to whine and whimper? Let every man that has an ounce of strength in him get up and put it forth in Heaven's name, and labour that his "soul may live."

Of this enormous Babel of a place I can give you no

account in writing: it is like the heart of all the universe; and the flood of human effort rolls out of it and into it with a violence that almost appals one's very sense. Paris scarcely occupies a quarter of the ground, and does not seem to have the twentieth part of the business. O that our father saw Holborn in a fog! with the black vapour brooding over it, absolutely like fluid ink; and coaches and wains and sheep and oxen and wild people rushing on with bellowings and shrieks and thundering din, as if the earth in general were gone distracted. To-day I chanced to pass through Smithfield, when the market was three-fourths over. I mounted the steps of a door, and looked abroad upon the area, an irregular space of perhaps thirty acres in extent, encircled with old dingy brick-built houses, and intersected with wooden pens for the cattle. What a scene! Innumerable herds of fat oxen, tied in long rows, or passing at a trot to their several shambles; and thousands of graziers, drovers, butchers, cattle-brokers with their quilted frocks and long goads pushing on the hapless beasts; hurrying to and fro in confused parties, shouting, jostling, cursing, in the midst of rain and *shairn*, and braying discord such as the imagination cannot figure. Then there are stately streets and squares, and calm green recesses to which nothing of this abomination is permitted to enter. No wonder Cobbett calls the place a Wen. It is a monstrous Wen! The thick smoke of it beclouds a space of thirty square miles; and a million of vehicles, from the dog- or cuddy-barrow to the giant waggon, grind along its streets for ever. I saw a six-horse wain the other day with, I think, number 200,000 and odds upon it!

There is an excitement in all this, which is pleasant as a transitory feeling, but much against my taste as a permanent one. I had much rather visit London from time to time, than live in it. There is in fact no *right* life in it that I can find: the people are situated here like plants in a hot-house, to which the quiet influences of sky and earth are never in their unadulterated state admitted. It is the case with all ranks; the carman with his huge slouch-hat hanging half-way down his back, consumes his breakfast of bread and tallow or hog's lard, sometimes as he swags along the streets, always in a hurried and precarious fashion, and supplies the deficit by continual pipes, and pots of beer. The fashionable lady rises at three in the afternoon, and begins to live towards midnight. Between these two extremes, the same false and tumultuous manner of existence more or less infests all ranks. It seems as if you were for ever in "an inn," the feeling of *home* in our acceptation of the term is not known to one of a thousand. You are packed into paltry shells of brick-houses (calculated to endure for forty years, and then fall); every door that slams to in the street is audible in your most secret chamber; the necessaries of life are hawked about through multitudes of hands, and reach you, frequently adulterated, always at rather more than *twice* their cost elsewhere; people's friends must visit them by rule and measure; and when you issue from your door, you are assailed by vast shoals of quacks, and showmen, and streetsweepers, and pickpockets, and mendicants of every degree and shape, all plying in noise or silent craft their several vocations, all in their hearts like "lions ravening for their prey." The blackguard population of the place is the most consummately blackguard of anything I ever saw.

Yet the people are in general a frank, jolly, *well-living*, kindly people. You get a certain way in their good graces with great ease: they want little more with you than now and then a piece of recreating conversation, and you are quickly on terms for giving and receiving it. Farther, I suspect, their nature or their habits seldom carry or admit them. I have found one or two strange mortals, whom I sometimes stare to see myself beside. There is Crabb Robinson, an old Templar (Advocate dwelling in the Temple), who gives me coffee and *Sally-Lunns* (a sort of buttered roll), and German books, and talk by the gallon in a minute. His windows look into — Alsatia! With the Montagus I, once a week or so, step in and chat away a friendly hour: they are good clever people, though their goodness and cleverness are strangely mingled with absurdity in word and deed. They like me very well: I saw Badams there last night; I am to see him more at large to-morrow or soon after. Mrs. Strachey has twice been here to see me — in her carriage, a circumstance of strange omen to our worthy [friend]. . . . Among the Poets I see Procter and Allan Cunningham as often as I like: the other night I had a second and much longer talk with Campbell. I went over with one Macbeth, not the "Usurper," but a hapless Preacher from Scotland, whose gifts, coupled with their drawbacks, cannot earn him bread in London, though Campbell and Irving and many more are doing all they can for him. Thomas is a clever man, and we had a much more pleasant conversation than our first; but I do not think my view of him was materially altered. He is vain and dry in heart; the brilliancy of his mind (which will not dazzle you to death after all) is like the glitter of an iceberg in the Greenland seas; parts of it are beautiful, but it is cold, cold, and you would rather look at it than touch it. I partly feel for Campbell: his early life was a tissue of wretchedness (here in London he has lived upon a pennyworth of milk and a penny roll per day); and at length his soul has got encrusted as with a case of iron; and he has betaken himself to sneering and selfishness — a common issue!

Irving I see as frequently and kindly as ever. His church and boy occupy him much. The *madness* of his popularity is altogether over; and he must content himself with playing a much lower game than he once anticipated; nevertheless I imagine he will do much good in London, where many men like him are greatly wanted. His wife and he are always good to me.

Respecting my future movements I can predict nothing certain yet. It is not improbable, I think, that I may see you all in Scotland before many weeks are come and gone. Here at any rate, in my present circumstances I do not mean to stay: it is expensive beyond measure (two guineas a week or thereby for the mere items of bed and board); and I must have a *permanent* abode of some kind devised for myself, if I mean to do any good. Within reach of Edinburgh or London, it matters little which. You have not yet determined upon leaving or retaining Mainhill? I think it is a pity that you had not some more kindly spot: at all events a better house I *would* have. Is Mainholm let? By clubbing our capitals together we might make something of it. A house in the country, and a horse to ride on, I must and will have if it be possible. Tell me all your views on these things when you write.

. . . Good night! my dear Alick! — I am, ever your affectionate Brother, T. CARLYLE

III

January 8, 1825

MY DEAR ALICK, — Your letter came to me the day before Christmas; it is time that it were answered. I am much obliged to you for your punctuality; a virtue which in my situation I am called upon to rival or even to surpass. I have no news for you; only harmless chat; but that and the assurance that there is no *bad* news will repay you for the charge of postage. . . .

Everything goes on with me here very much as it was doing when I wrote last. . . . I think I have well-nigh decided on returning to Scotland, when this Book is off my hands. This tumultuous capital is not the place for one like me. The very expense of it were almost enough to drive me out of it: I cannot live in the simplest style under about two guineas a week; a sum that would suffice to keep a decent roof of my own above me in my Fatherland. Besides I ought to settle somewhere, and get a home and neighbourhood among my fellow-creatures. Now this London, to my mind, is not a flattering scene for such an enterprise. One hates, for one thing, to be a *foreigner* anywhere; and this, after all that can be said about it, is the case with *every* Scotchman in this city. They live as aliens here, unrooted in the soil; without political, religious, or even much social, interest in the community, distinctly feeling every day that with them it is money only that can "make the mare to go." Hence cash! cash! cash! is the everlasting cry of their souls. They are consequently very "hard characters"; they believe in nothing but their ledgers; their precept is like that of Iago, "Put money in your purse"; or as he of Burnfoot more emphatically expressed it, "Now, Jock! Get siller, honestly, if thou can; but ony way *get* it!" I should like but indifferently to be ranked among them; for my sentiments and theirs are not at all germane. The first *improvement* they make upon themselves in the South is to acquire the habit of sneering at their honest old country; vending many stale jokes about its poverty, and the happiness of travelling with one's face *towards* the sun. This is a "damnable heresy," as honest Allan Cunningham called it. I have no patience with the leaden-hearted dogs. Often when appealed to that I might confirm such shallow sarcasms, I have risen in my wrath, and branded them with my bitterest contempt. But here they are staple speculation with our degenerate compatriots. BULL himself, again, though a frank, beef-loving, joyous kind of person, *is* excessively stupid: take him out of the sphere of the *five senses*, and he gazes with a vacant astonishment, and wondering "what the devil the fellow *can* mean." This is comparatively the state of all ranks, so far as I have seen them, from the highest to the lowest; but especially of the latter. Of these it is unspeakably so! Yesterday I went to see Newgate, under the auspices of the benevolent Mrs. Fry, a Quaker lady who every Friday goes on her errand of mercy to inspect the condition of the female prisoners. She, this good Quakeress, is as much like an angel of Peace as any person I ever saw: she read a chapter, and *expounded* it, to the most degraded audience of the universe, in a style of beautiful simplicity which I shall not soon forget. But oh! the male felons! the two hundred polluted wretches, through whose stalls and yards I was next carried! There were they of all climates and kinds, the Jew, the Turk, the "Christian"; from the gray villain of sixty to the blackguard boy of *eight!* Nor was it their depravity that struck me, so much as their debasement. Most of them actually looked like *animals;* you could see no traces of a *soul* (not even of a bad one) in their gloating, callous, sensual countenances; they had never *thought* at all, they had only eaten and drunk and made merry. I have seen as wicked people in the north; but it was another and far less abominable sort of wickedness. A Scotch blackguard is very generally a thinking reasoning person; some theory and principle of life, a satanical philosophy, beams from every feature of his rugged scowling countenance. Not so here. The sharpness of these people was the cunning of a fox, their stubbornness was the sullen gloom of a mastiff. Newgate holds, I believe, within its walls more human baseness than any other spot in the Creation.

But why do I write of it or aught connected with it, since in a few weeks I hope to tell you everything by word of mouth? We are on the fifteenth sheet of *Schiller; six* more will see us through it. The moment it is finished, I purpose to decamp. I have given the creatures *four* weeks (they engage for *three*) to settle everything: I should not be surprised if you met me at the Candlemas Fair on the Plainstones of Dumfries! Soon after the beginning of February I do expect to see old, meagre but true-hearted Annandale again. No doubt, you will have the *wark-gear afoot*, that is, the pony in riding order, and everything in readiness for me. When arrived, my purposes are various, and inviting though unsettled. I have written to Edinburgh about a projected translation of *Schiller's Works;* Brewster sends me word that Blackwood (the Bookseller) "has no doubt he will be able to engage with me, in *Schiller* (which, however, he does not seem to relish), or in some other literary object." Blackwood, I believe, is but a knave; and I put no faith in him. Nay, since I began to write this sentence, I have a letter from the scoundrel Boyd "respectfully declining" to engage in that speculation of *Schiller!* So that I rather suppose *it* must be renounced. No matter! There are plenty more where it came from! I am bent on *farming*, for the recovery of my health; nay "marriage" itself is sometimes not out of my ulterior contemplations! But I will explain all things when we meet.

. . . .

But the day is breaking up into fair sunshine; and I must out to take the benefit of it. Let me have a letter from you, a long one, and a good one like the last, by the very earliest opportunity. Thank my kind true Mother for her note: tell her it will not be long till I answer all her queries by word of mouth. In the meantime, I have a message for her, which I know will please her well, because it is to *do something for me.* Badams prescribes *warmth* above all things: he made me wear close stocking (flannel or rather woollen) drawers even in summer. My Mother once offered to get Peter Little to work me such a pair; tell her that now if she has any wool, I will take them. If she has not, she need never mind in the least: we can settle it, — when — we meet! Do you regularly hear of Jack? He is a letter in my debt for ten days. But I hope the good soul is well. Does he send you the *Examiner?* Has he written you a translation of Goethe's letter to me? I was very glad to hear from the old blade, in so kind though so brief a fashion. I mean to send him a copy of *Schiller's Life*, as soon as it is ready.

Now, my dear Boy, I must take my flight. I have purchased me a small seal and the Carlyles' crest with *Humiliate* and all the rest of it engraven on it. The thing lies at present in Oxford Street, and was to be ready about this time to-day. I am going thither: if I get it, I will seal this letter with it, for your edification. Write directly, and tell me all; the progress of the *Gheen* and everything notable, in and about Mainhill. The smallest incident from that quarter recorded in your pithy style is valuable to me.

Irving and I are as friendly as ever. He is toiling in the midst of many difficulties and tasks, internal and external, domestic and ecclesiastic. I wish him well through them! He is the best man I have met in England. But here, as I told him lately, he has no home; he is a "missionary" rather than a pastor. — My Father has never written to me: I should like much to see his hand in London. Give my warmest love to him and Mother, and all the *brethren* and sisters, beginning with Mag and ending with Jenny. Write soon, good Alick! — I am, ever your true brother,

T. Carlyle

XII

PARTICULAR WIFE TO PARTICULAR HUSBAND

(With Thomas Carlyle's Notes)

I

Jane Welsh to Thomas Carlyle ~ ~ ~

October 12, 1835

DEAREST, — A newspaper is very pleasant when one is expecting nothing at all; but when it comes in place of a letter it is a positive insult to one's feelings. Accordingly your first newspaper was received by me in choicest mood; and the second would have been pitched in the fire, had there been one at hand, when, after having tumbled myself from top story at the risk of my neck, I found myself deluded with "wun penny 'm." However, I flatter myself you would experience something of a similar disappointment on receiving mine; and so we are quits, and I need not scold you. I have not been a day in bed since you went — have indeed been almost free of headache, and all other aches; and everybody says Mrs. Carlyle begins to look better — and what everybody says must be true. With this improved health everything becomes tolerable, even to the peesweep Sereetha (for we are still without other help). Now that I do not see you driven desperate with the chaos, I can take a quiet view of it, and even reduce it to some degree of order. Mother and I have fallen naturally into a fair division of labour, and we keep a very tidy house. Sereetha has attained the unhoped-for perfection of getting up at half after six of her own accord, lighting the parlour-fire, and actually placing the breakfast things *nil desperandum me duce!* I get up half after seven, and prepare the coffee, and bacon-ham (which is the life of me, making me always hungrier the more I eat of it). Mother, in the interim, makes her bed, and sorts her room. After breakfast, mother descends to the inferno, where she jingles and scours, and from time to time scolds Sereetha till all is right and tight there. I, above stairs, sweep the parlour, blacken the grate — make the room look cleaner than it has been since the days of Grace Macdonald[1]; then mount aloft to make my own bed (for I was resolved to enjoy the privilege of having a bed of my own); then clean myself (as the servants say), and sit down to the Italian lesson. A bit of meat roasted at the oven suffices two days cold, and does not plague us with cookery. Sereetha can fetch up tea-things, and the porridge is easily made on the parlour-fire; the kitchen one being allowed to go out (for economy), when the Peesweep retires to bed at eight o'clock.

That we are not neglected by the public, you may infer from the fact that, this very night, Peesweep fetched up four tea-cups on the tray; and when I asked the meaning of the two additional, she inquired, with surprise, "Were there to be no gentlemen?" "In fact, the kindness of these people" "beats the world." I had some

[1] The Edinburgh servant we brought with us to Craigenputtock; the skilfullest we ever had anywhere.

private misgiving that your men would not mind me when you were not here, and I should have been mortified in that case, though I could not have blamed them. But it is quite the reverse. Little Grant[1] has been twice to know if he could "do anything for me." Garnier has been twice! The first time by engagement to you; the second time to meet Pepoli, whom he knew in Paris, and wished to re-know, and who proved *perfido* on the occasion. Pepoli has been twice, and is gliding into a flirtation with — *mia madre!* who presented him, in a manner *molto graziosa*, with her tartan scarf. From John Mill I have been privileged with two notes, and one visit. He evidently tried to yawn as little as possible, and stayed till the usual hour, lest, I suppose, he should seem to have missed your conversation. John Sterling and the Stimabile,[2] of course. The latter was at tea last night to meet Mr. Gibson[3] — one of my fatal attempts at producing a reunion, for they coincided in nothing but years. The Stimabile was at Brighton for several days, and goes again next week, so that he has not been too deadly frequent.

Our visiting has been confined to one dinner and two teas at the Sterling's, and a tea at Hunt's! You must know, —— came the day after you went, and stayed two days. As she desired above all things to see Hunt, I

[1] Official in the India House, a friend and admirer of John Mill's.

[2] A title we had for John's father. Signora degli Antoni, the Italian instructress in these months, setting her pupil an epistolary pattern, had thrown off one day a billet as if addressed to Edward Sterling, which began with *Stimabile Signor*.

[3] Was a massive, easy, friendly, dull person, physically one of the best washed I ever saw; American merchant, "who had made, and again lost, three fortunes"; originally a Nithsdale pedlar boy, "Black Wull," by title; "Silver-headed Packman," he was often called here.

wrote him a note asking him if I might bring her up to call. He replied he was just setting off to town, but would look in at eight o'clock. I supposed this, as usual, a mere put-off; but he actually came and found Pepoli as well as Miss ——, was amazingly lively, and very lasting, for he stayed till near twelve. Between ourselves, it gave me a poorish opinion of him, to see how uplifted to the third heaven he seemed by ——'s compliments and sympathising talk. He asked us all, with enthusiasm, to tea the following Monday. —— came on purpose and slept here. He sang, talked like a pea-gun[1] ever to ——, who drank it all in like nectar, while my mother looked cross enough, and I had to listen to the whispered confidences of Mrs. Hunt. But for me, who was declared to be grown "quite prim and elderly," I believe they would have communicated their mutual experiences in a retired window-seat till morning. "God bless you, Miss ——," was repeated by Hunt three several times in tones of ever-increasing pathos and tenderness as he handed her downstairs behind me. ——, for once in her life, seemed past speech. At the bottom of the stairs a demur took place. I saw nothing; but I heard, with my wonted glegness — what think you? — a couple of handsome smacks! and then an almost inaudibly soft "God bless you, Miss ——!"

Now just remember what sort of looking woman is —— ; and figure their transaction! If he had kissed me, it would have been intelligible, but ——, of all people! By the way, Mr. Craik[2] is immensely delighted with you, and grateful to Susan for having brought you together.

[1] *Scoticè*, gun made of grill-barrel for shooting peas (and "cracking," which also means pleasantly conversing).

[2] *Useful Knowledge* Craik, poor fellow!

Mrs. Cole [1] came the other day, and sat an hour waiting for me while I was out, and finally had to go, leaving an obliging note offering me every assistance in procuring a servant.

Mrs. John Sterling takes to me wonderfully; but John, I perceive, will spoil all with his innocence. He told her the other day, when she was declaring her wish that he would write on Theology rather than make verses, that she "might fight out that matter with Mrs. Carlyle, who, he knew, was always on the side of the poetical." He (Sterling) has written a positively splendid poem of half-an-hour's length — an allegorical shadowing of the union of the ideal and actual. It is far the best thing he ever did — far beyond anything I could have supposed him capable of. He said, when he was writing it, he thought sometimes, "Carlyle will be pleased with that."

To descend to the practical, or, I should rather say ascend, for I have filled my whole paper with mere gossip. I think you seem, so far as human calculations avail, to have made a good hit as to the servant; character is not worth a straw; but, you say she looks intelligent and good-humoured, is young and willing.[2] Fetch her, then, in God's name, and I will make the best I can of her. After all, we fret ourselves too much about little things; much that might be laughed off, if one were well and cheerful as one ought to be, becomes a grave affliction from being too gravely looked at. Remember also meal, and oh, for goodness sake, procure a dozen of bacon-hams! There is no bottom to my appetite for them. Sell poor Harry, by all means,

[1] The now thrice-notable "Crystal Palace," "Brompton Boilers," etc., etc., Henry Cole's wife.

[2] Anne Cook (got for me by sister Mary, at Annan).

or shoot him. We are too poor to indulge our fine feelings with keeping such large pets (especially at other people's expense). What a pity no frank is to be got! I have told you nothing yet. No word ever came from Basil Montagu. I have translated four songs into Italian — written a long excessively *spirituosa* letter to "mia adorabile Clementina,"[1] and many *graziose cartucie* besides. In truth, I have a divine *ingegno!*

You will come back strong and cheerful, will you not? I wish you were come, anyhow. Don't take much castor; eat plenty of chicken broth rather. Dispense my love largely. Mother returns your kiss with interest. We go on tolerably enough; but she has vowed to hate all my people except Pepoli. So that there is ever a "dark brown shadd" in all my little reunions. She has given me a glorious black-velvet gown, realising my *beau idéal* of Putz.

Did you take away my folding penknife? We are knifeless here. We were to have gone to Richmond to-day with the Silverheaded; but, to my great relief, it turned out that the steamboat is not running.

God keep you, my own dear husband, and bring you safe back to me. The house looks very empty without you, and my mind feels empty too. —

Your JANE

II

August 23, 1842

MY DEAR HUSBAND, — The pen was in my hand to write yesterday; but nothing would have come out of me yesterday except "literature of desperation";[2]

[1] Degli Antoni.

[2] *Litterature der Verzweiflung* was Goethe's definition of Victor Hugo and Co.'s new gospel.

and, aware of this, I thought it better to hold my peace for the next twenty-four hours, till a new night had either habilitated me for remaining awhile longer, or brought me to the desperate resolution of flying home for my life. Last night, Heaven be thanked, went off peaceably; and to-day I am in a state to record my last trial, without danger of becoming too tragical, or alarming you with the prospect of my making an unseemly termination of my visit. (Oh, what pens!)

To begin where I left off. On Sunday, after writing to you, I attended the afternoon service! Regy looked so *wae* when I answered his question "whether I was going?" in the negative, that a weak pity induced me to revise my determination. "It is a nice pew, that of ours," said old Mr. Buller; "it suits me remarkably well, for being so deep I am not overlooked; and in virtue of that, I read most part of the *Femme de Qualité* this morning!" "But don't," he added, "tell Mr. Regy this! Had Theresa been there, I would not have done it, for I like to set a good example!" I also turned the depth of the pew to good account; when the sermon began, I made myself, at the bottom of it, a sort of Persian couch out of the praying-cushions; laid off my bonnet, and stretched myself out very much at my ease. I seemed to have been thus just one drowsy minute when a slight rustling, and the words "Now to Father, Son, and Holy Ghost," warned me to put on my bonnet, and made me for the first time aware that I had been asleep! For the rest, the music that day ought to have satisfied me; for it seemed to have remodelled itself expressly to suit my taste — Scotch tunes, produced with the nasal discordant emphasis of a Scotch country-congregation, and no clarinet. I noticed in a little square gallery-seat, the only one in the church, a portly character, who acts as blacksmith, sitting with a wand, some five feet long, in his hand, which he swayed about majestically as if it had been a sceptre! On inquiring of our man-servant what this could possibly mean or symbolise, he informed me it was "to beat bad children." "And are the children here so bad they need such a functionary?" "Ah, they will always, them little 'uns, be doing mischief in the church: it's a-wearisome for the poor things, and the rod keeps them in fear!"

In the evening, the drive, as always, with this only difference, that on Sunday evenings, Mr. Buller only walks the horse, from principle! After this conscientious exercising, the game at chess! My head had ached more or less all day, and I was glad to get to bed, where I was fortunate enough to get to sleep without any violent disturbance. The next day, however, my head was rather worse than better; so that I would fain have "declined from"[1] calling on Lady Agnes; but Mrs. Buller was bent on going to Livermere, and so, as I did not feel up to walking, it was my only chance of getting any fresh air and exercise that day. To Livermere we went then, before dinner, the dinner being deferred till five o'clock to suit the more fashionable hours of our visitees. "The Pagets" seem to be extremely like other mortals, neither better nor bonnier nor wiser. To do them justice, however, they might, as we found them, have been sitting for a picture of high life doing the amiable and the rural in the country. They had placed a table under the shadow of a beech-tree; and at this sat Mr. Byng studying the "Examiner"; Lady Agnes reading —

[1] The phrase of a rustic cousin of ours, kind of a solemn pedant in his way.

"Oh, nothing at all, only some nonsense that Lord Londonderry has been printing; I cannot think what has tempted him;" and a boy and girl marking for a cricket-party, consisting of all the men-servants, and two older little sons, who were playing for the entertainment of their master and mistress and their own; the younger branches ever and anon clapping their hands, and calling out "What fun!" I may mention for your consolation that Mr. Byng (a tall, gentlemanly, blasé-looking man) was dressed from head to foot in unbleached linen; while Babbie may take a slight satisfaction to her curiosity *de femme* from knowing how a Paget attires herself of a morning, to sit under a beech-tree — a white-flowered muslin pelisse, over pale blue satin; a black lace scarf fastened against her heart with a little gold horse-shoe; her white neck tolerably revealed, and set off with a brooch of diamonds; immense gold bracelets and immense gold chain; a little white silk bonnet with a profusion of blond and flowers; thus had she prepared herself for being rural. But, with all this finery, she looked a good-hearted, rattling, clever *haveral*[1] sort of a woman. Her account of Lord Londonderry's sentimental dedication to his wife was perfect — "from a goose to a goose!" — and she defended herself with her pocket handkerchief against the wasps, with an energy. When we had sat sufficiently long under the tree, Mrs. Buller asked her to take me through the gardens, which she did very politely, and gave me some carnations and verbenas; and then through the stables, which were, indeed, the finer sight of the two.

[1] Good-humoured foolish person. I should not wonder if it came from Avril (which in old Scotch is corrupted into Averil, and even Haver Hill), and had originally meant "April fool."

All this sight-seeing, however, did not help my head; at night I let the chess go as it liked; took some medicine, and went early to bed, determined to be well on the morrow. About twelve, I fell into a sound sleep, out of which I was startled by the tolling of the church-bell. The church, you remember, is only a stone-cast from the house; so that, when the bell tolls, one seems to be exactly under its tongue. I sprang up — it was half after three by my watch — hardly light; the bell went on to toll two loud dismal strokes at regular intervals of a minute. What could it be? I fancied fire — fancied insurrection. I ran out into the passage and listened at Regy's door, all was still; then I listened at Mrs. Buller's, I heard her cough; surely, I thought, since she is awake, she would ring her bell if there were anything alarming for her in this tolling, it must be some other noise of the many they "have grown used to." So I went to bed again, but, of course, could not get another wink of sleep all night; for the bell only ceased tolling at my ear about six in the morning, and then I was too nervous to avail myself of the silence. "What on earth was the bell?" I asked Regy the first thing in the morning. "Oh, that was only the passing-bell! It was ordered to be rung during the night for an old lady who died the night before." This time, however, I had the satisfaction of seeing Mrs. Buller as angry as myself; for she also had been much alarmed.

Of course, yesterday I was quite ill, with the medicine, the sleeplessness, and the fright; and I thought I really could not stay any longer in a place where one is liable to such alarms. But now, as usual, one quiet night has given me hopes of more; and it would be a pity to return worse than I went away. I do not seem to myself to be nearly done; but Mr. Buller is sitting at my elbow with the chess-board, saying, "When you are ready I am ready." I am ready. Love to Babbie; I have your and her letter; but *must* stop.

III

September 13, 1844

DEAREST, — I have absolutely no composure of soul for writing just now. The fact is, I have undertaken far more this time than human discretion would have dreamt of putting into one week; knowing your horror of sweeps and carpet-beaters and "all that sort of thing," I would, in my romantic self-devotion, sweep all the chimneys and lift all the carpets before you came; and had you arrived this day, as you first proposed, you would have found me still in a regular mess, threatening to thicken into "immortal smash." But by Thursday I hope to have "got everything satisfactorily arranged," as poor Plattnauer is always saying.

And there have been so many other things to take me up, besides the sweeps, etc. Almost every evening somebody has been here. The evening of the Bullers' departure Jenkin's Hen [1] came, pale as a candle, with a red circle round each eye which was very touching; — he had evidently been crying himself quite sick and sore. Lady Lewis [2] had invited him to dine with her; but, "he could not go there, he could not eat any dinner, he was afraid to go home to his own silent house — he thought I could understand his feelings, and so had come to pass the evening with me." What a gift of understanding

[1] Fleming. To "die the death of Jenkin's hen" expressed, in Annandale, the maximum of pusillanimity.

[2] The late C. Buller's aunt.

other people's feelings I am supposed to have — *moi!* Oh, my dear, the cat produced two kittens in your bed this morning, and we have drowned them — and now she also thinks I can understand her feelings, and is coming about my feet mewing in a way that quite wrings my heart. Poor thing! I never saw her take on so badly before.

Well! but on Saturday night Helen had just gone to seek sugar for the tea when a rap came, which I preferred answering myself to allowing Plattnauer to answer it, and — oh Heavens! — what should I see in the dark opening? A little human phenomenon, in a triple-cornered hat! Bishop ****** again! I screamed, a good, genuine, horrified scream! Whereupon he stept in — and, as the devil would have it — on my bad toe! and then I uttered a series of screams which made Plattnauer savage with him for the rest of the evening. He had come up to seek himself a new assistant, the old one being promoted. There is no end to his calls to London! But he was plainly mortally afraid of Plattnauer, who as good as told him he was "one of the windbags," and will not trouble us again I think while he is here.

Yesterday afternoon came Henry Taylor, but only for a few minutes; he had been unexpectedly "turned adrift on our shores," and could only wait till a Wandsworth steamer should come up. I was very kind to him and he looked as if he could have kissed me for being glad to see him — oh, how odd! I put on my bonnet and went with him to the boat; and he complimented me on going out without gloves or shawl. I was the first woman he had ever found in this world who could go out of her house without at least a quarter of an hour's preparation! They have taken a house at Mortlake, near Richmond.

But there is no possibility of telling you all the things I have to tell at this writing. They will keep till you come. Only let me not forget to say there is an American letter come for John, which I send on by this day's post.

Your letter, written apparently on Saturday, was not read by me till yesterday afternoon; the postman came so long after twelve when I had been under the imperative necessity to go out. Give my love to Mr. Baring. — Ever your distracted

GOODY

IV

July 23, 1845

DEAREST, — It is all as well as could be expected. I arrived without accident, not even much tired, an hour and a half before I was looked for — in fact between five and six. Consequently there was nobody to meet me, and I had some difficulty in getting myself a car, and at the same time keeping watch over my trunk and dressing-box; the former indeed was getting itself coolly borne away by a porter amongst some other people's luggage, when I laid my hand on it, and indicated: Thus far shalt thou go but no farther. My uncle I met tumbling downstairs, with what speed he might, prepared for being kissed to death; then came Maggie; and lastly Babbie, flushed and embarrassed, and unsatisfactory looking; for, alas! she had been all day preserving strawberries, and had not expected me so soon, and was not dressed: to be an unwise virgin, taken with one's lamp untrimmed, means here to be caught in *dêshabillé*. A —— I have not seen yet — *tant mieux*, for I don't like him "the least in the world." Johnnie has sunk away into "an unintelligible whinner." [1]

[1] Some fool's speech to me, I forget whose.

On the whole there is little "food for the young soul, Mr. Carlyle!" But *she* (as Mazzini insists on calling the soul, and I think with reason; making the soul into an *it* being — what shall I say? — a desecration, upon my honour) — "she" can do without visible food, like my leech, for all the while "she" is to abide in the place. And "one has always one's natural affections left." And then "to give pleasure to others!" The compensation that lies in that under all circumstances! Ah!

I am established in Mary's little room (off my uncle's) which they have made as tidy as possible for me. There is a tradition of "a little wee wifie that lived in a shoe"; but I am still more curiously lodged, for this room is for all the world like a boot, the bed occupying the heel of it, a little bed like a coffin.

In so new a predicament, of course I could not sleep; the best I made of it was a doze from time to time of a few minutes' duration, from which I started up with a sensation of horror, like what must have been felt by the victim of the Iron Shroud. For the rest, there was a cat opera, in which the *prima donna* had an organ that "bet the worl";[1] then there are some half-dozen of stout-lunged cocks, and a dog that lyrically recognises every passing event. Perhaps, like the pigs, I shall get used to it; if not I must just go all the sooner to Seaforth where there is at least a certain quiet.

My coachful of men turned out admirably, as silent as could be wished, yet not deficient in the courtesies of life. The old gentleman with moustachios and a red face was Colonel Cleveland, of the Artillery, "much distinguished in the wars." There was another old

[1] Annandale for "beat the world."

gentleman still more miraculous than Rio;[1] for he had one eye boiled, the other parboiled, no leg, and his mind boiled to jelly, and yet he got to Liverpool just as well as the rest of us. The little man opposite me, who was absorbed in Eugene Sue's female Bluebeard, was a German, and, pleased to see me reading his language, he gave me his pea-jacket to wrap my legs in, for we were all perished with cold. The English dandy with the heaven-blue waistcoat slept the whole way, exactly in the attitude of "James" waiting for the Sylphide to come and kiss him; but he might sleep long enough, I fancy, before any "bit of fascination" would take the trouble.

And now you must "excuse us the day." After such a night, I can neither "make wits,"[2] nor, what were more to the purpose, senses, for your gratification. I shall go and walk, and look at the *Great Britain* packet; if one does not enlighten one's mind in the shipping department here, I see not how else one shall enlighten it.

Babbie has just knocked to beg I would give her love to you, and most sincere thanks for the Book,[3] the preface of which I read aloud to my uncle at breakfast; and he pronounced it "very satirical" — a true speak!

God bless you, dear. I do not wish you to feel lonely, nor will you; and yet I should not precisely like if you missed me none at all. — Your distracted

JANEKIN

[1] Rio, a wandering, rather loud and headlong, but innocent-hearted, French friend, Neo-Catholic, etc., I believe is still living in Paris; a stranger here for twenty-five years now.

[2] Bölte's phrase for the sad operation of being with effort "witty."

[3] "Book," I suppose, will be *Life of Schiller*, 2nd edition.

V

August 16, 1845

DEAREST, — I never know whether a letter is welcomer when it arrives after having been impatiently waited for, or like yesterday's, "quite promiscuously," when I was standing on the broad basis of "Blessed are they who do not hope, for they shall not be disappointed!" I assure you I am not the only person obliged by your writing; it makes a very palpable difference in my amiability throughout the day whether I have a letter to begin it with.

Last night we went, according to programme, to Mrs. A——'s and "it's but fair to state" that the drive there and back in the moonlight was the best of it. The party did me no ill, however; it was not a Unitarian crush like the last, but adapted to the size of the room: select, moreover, and with the crowning grace of an open window. There was an old gentleman who did the impossible to inspire me with a certain respect: Y—— they called him, and his glory consists in owning the Prince's Park, and throwing it open to "poors." Oh, what a dreadful little old man! He plied me with questions, and suggestions about you, till I was within a trifle of "putting my finger in the pipy o' im."[1] "How did Mr. Carlyle treat Oliver Cromwell's crimes?" "His what?" said I. "The atrocities he exercised on the Irish." "Oh, you mean massacring a garrison or two? All that is treated very briefly." "But Mr. Carlyle must feel a just horror of it." "Horror? Oh, none at all, I assure you! He regards it as the only means under the circumstances to

[1] Crying baby unappeasable. "Put your finger in ta pipie o't" (little windpipe,) said some Highland body.

save blood-shed." The little old gentleman bounced back in his chair, and spread out his two hands, like a duck about to swim, while there burst from his lips a groan that made everyone look at us. What had I said to their Mr. Y——? By-and-by the old gentleman returned to the charge. "Mr. Carlyle must be feeling much delighted about the Academical Schools?" "Oh no, he has been so absorbed in his own work lately that he has not been at leisure to be delighted about anything." "But, madam! a man may attend to his own work, and attend at the same time to questions of great public interest." "Do you think so? I don't." Another bounce on the chair. Then, with a sort of awe, as of a "demon more wicked than your wife"[1] "Do you not think, madam, that more good might be done by taking up the history of the actual time than of past ages? Such a time as this, so full of improvements in arts and sciences, the whole face of Europe getting itself changed! Suppose Mr. Carlyle should bring out a yearly volume about all this?" This was Y——'s last flight of eloquence with me, for catching the eyes of a lady (your Miss L—— of "The Gladiator") fixed on me with the most ludicrous expression of sympathy, I fairly burst out laughing till the tears ran down; and when I had recovered myself, the old gentleman had turned for compensation to J. M——. J. had reasons for being civil to him which I had not, Mr. Y—— being his landlord; but he seemed to be answering him in his sleep while his waking thoughts were intent on an empty chair betwixt Geraldine and myself, and eventually he made it his own. As if to deprecate my confounding him with these

[1] Peter Nimmo's sermon on Ananias and Sapphira: "Tempted by some demon more wicked than his wife."

Y——'s, he immediately began to speak in the most disrespectful manner of Mechanics' Institutes "and all that sort of thing"; and then we got on these eternal Vestiges of Creation,[1] which he termed, rather happily, "animated mud." Geraldine and Mrs. Paulet were wanting to engage him in a doctrinal discussion, which they are extremely fond of: "Look at Jane," suddenly exclaimed Geraldine, "she is quizzing us in her own mind. You must know" (to Mr. M——) "we cannot get Jane to care a bit about doctrines." "I should think not," said M——, with great vivacity; "Mrs. Carlyle is the most concrete woman that I have seen for a long while." "Oh," said Geraldine, "she puts all her wisdom into practice, and so never gets into scrapes." "Yes," said M—— in a tone significant of much, "to keep out of doctrines is the only way to keep out of scrapes." Was not that a creditable speech in a Unitarian?

Miss L—— is a frank, rather agreeable, woman, forty or thereabouts, who looks as if she had gone through a good deal of hardship; not "a domineering genius" by any means,[2] but with sense enough for all practical purposes, such as admiring you to the skies, and Cromwell too. The rest of the people were "chiefly musical, Mr. Carlyle." Mrs. A—— is very much fallen off in her singing since last year; I suppose from squalling so much to her pupils. She is to dine here to-day, and ever so many people besides, to meet those R——s. Doubtless we shall be "borne through with an honourable throughbearing"; [3] but quietness is best.

[1] Dull Book (quasi-atheistic), much talked of then.

[2] Jeffrey? "Pooh! clever enough, but not a domineering genius!" (Poor Gray of the High School, Edinburgh, thirty years before.)

[3] Burgher minister's thanksgiving on a Sacramental occasion.

And now I must go and walk, while the sun shines. Our weather here is very showery and cold. I heard a dialogue the other morning betwixt Mr. Paulet and his factotum, which amused me much. The factotum was mowing the lawn. Mr. Paulet threw up the breakfast-room window, and called to him: "Knolles! how looks my wheat?" "Very distressed indeed, sir." "Are we much fallen down?" "No, sir, but we are black, very black." "All this rain, I should have thought, would have made us fall down?" "Where the crops are heavy they are a good deal laid, sir, but it would take a vast of rain to lay us." "Oh, then, Knolles, it is because we are not powerful enough that we are not fallen down?" "Sir?" "It is because we are not rich enough?" "Beg pardon, sir, but I don't quite understand?" Mr. Paulet shut the window and returned to his breakfast. God keep you, dear. — Your own J. C.

VI

August 5, 1852

YOU recollect, dear, that Macready told me of two routes, recommending that by Frome as the quickest and least fatiguing; so I rendered myself at the Paddington station on Friday morning, with my night things in a bag on one arm and my "blessed"[1] in a basket on the other. He gave me no trouble, kept himself hidden and motionless till the train started, and then looked out cautiously, as much as to say, "Are we safe?" The journey to Frome was quite a rest after that morning's work (carrying down all the books from the top landing-place into the back parlour), and

[1] Dog Nero.

I descended from the train quite fresh for the thirty miles by coach.

But when I inquired about the coach to Sherborne, I was told there was none. "A coach passing through Sherborne passed through Frome without coming to the station at eleven in the morning," three hours before the time we were at; "no other since many months back." My first thought was, "What a mercy you were not with me!" my next that the Macreadys could not blame me for keeping them waiting; and then I "considered," like the piper's cow, and resolved not to stay all day and night at Frome, but to take a Yeovil coach, which started at five, and which could take me, I was told, to a wayside inn within eight miles of Sherborne, and there I hoped to find a fly "or something." Meanwhile I would proceed to the town of Frome, a mile from the station, and get something to eat, and even to drink, "feeling it my duty" to keep my heart up by all needful appliances. I left my little bag at the station, where the coach came, and set my dog quite free, and we pursued our way as calmly and naturally as if we had known where we were going.

Frome is a dull, dirty-looking place, full of plumbers; one could fancy the Bennett controversy [1] must have been a godsend to it. I saw several inns, and chose "The George" for its name's sake. I walked in and asked to have some cold meat and a pint bottle of Guinness's porter. They showed me to an ill-aired parlour, and brought me some cold lamb that the flies had been buzzing round for a week — even Nero disdained to touch it. I ate bread, however, and drank all the porter; and

[1] Something in the newspaper.

"the cha-arge"[1] for that feeble refection was 2s. 6d.! Already I had paid one pound eight and sixpence for the train. It was going to be a most unexpectedly costly journey to me. But for that reflection I could almost have laughed at my forlorn position there.

The inn and town were "so disagreeable" that I went presently back to the station, preferring to wait there. One of the men who had informed me about the coach came to me, as I was sitting on a bench, and remarked on the beauty of the scene, especially of some scarlet beans that were growing in his own piece of garden. "Ah," he said, "I have lived in London, and I have lived abroad; I have been here and there, backwards and forwards, while I was in service with them as never could rest; but I am satisfied now that the only contentment for man is in growing his own VEGETABLE!" "Look at them beans," he said again. "Well, to-morrow they'll be ready, and I'll be pulling them, and boiling them, and eating them — and such a taste! No agriculture like that in Piccadilly!" Then he looked sympathisingly at me and said, "I'm going to get you something you'll like, and that's a glass of cool, fresh, clear water;" and he went away with a jug to his garden and fetched some water from a little spring well and a great handful of mignonette. "There! there's something sweet for you, and here's splendid water, that

[1] In my first voyage to London (1824, by Leith smack) a certain very rustic-looking, but polite and quiet old baronet, called Sir David Milne, slept in the same cabin with me; and there and on deck was an amusing study. Courteous, solemn, yet awkward, dull; chewing away the *r* when he spoke, which indeed was seldom, and then mainly in the way of economic inquiry to passengers who knew London — what you could do there, see, eat, etc.; and to every item, the farther question: "And what is the cha-arge (charge)?"

you won't find the like of in Piccadilly!" I asked him "how it was going with Mr. Bennett?" "Huh, I hear no complaints, but I goes to neither one nor other of them, and follows my own notions. I finds agriculture the thing!" He would have been worth a hundred pounds to Dickens, that man.

I had the coach all to myself for awhile; then a young gentleman got in, who did exactly the right thing by me, neither spoke to me nor looked at me till we stopped at Castle Carey (Yeovil is pronounced Youghal, Carey Carry. I grew quite frightened that I had been somehow transported into Ireland). There the young gentleman went into the inn, and said to me first, "Excuse the liberty I take in asking, but would you take anything — a little wine and water?" I thought that very polite; but I was to meet with "something more exquisite still" before I got to Sherborne. At the "Sparkford" Inn, eight miles from Sherborne, I got out and asked, had they a fly? "Yes, but one of its wheels was broken, and it was gone to be mended!" "Had they any other conveyance that was whole — a gig or cart?" "Yes, they had a nice little gig, and I should have the loan of a cloak to keep me warm" (the evening was rather chill). So I went in, and sat down in a parlour; where an old gentleman was finishing off with bread-and-cheese. He soon made himself master of my case, and regretted he was not going back to Sherborne that night, as then he would have taken me in his carriage; and presently he offered something else more practical, viz., to try to recover my parasol (my mother's, the one she bought with the sovereign you gave her,[1] and which I had got new covered), left stupidly on

[1] A sovereign to each of them, on returning home with a pocketful from my "first lecture." Ah, me!

the roof of the coach, and never recollected till the coach, with its four horses, had thundered past the window! If the landlady would tell the coachman about it next day, and get it there, he, the old gentleman, would bring it to Sherborne House. I went into the lobby to tell the landlady, some five or eight minutes after the coach had started, and told her, in presence of a gentleman, who was preparing to start in a barouchette with two horses. He looked hard at me, but said nothing; and a minute or two after I saw him drive past the window. Some twenty minutes after, I started myself, in a little gig, with a brisk little horse, and silent driver. Nothing could be more pleasant than so pirring through quiet roads, in the dusk, with the moon coming out. I felt as if I were reading about myself in a Miss Austen novel. But it got beyond Miss Austen when, at the end of some three miles, before a sort of carrier's inn, the gentleman of the barouchette stept into the middle of the road, making a sort of military signal to my driver, which he repeated with impatience when the man did not at once draw up! I sat confounded, expecting what he would do next. We had halted; the gentleman came to my side, and said, exactly as in a book: "Madam, I have the happiness of informing you that I have reclaimed your parasol; and it lies here in my carriage ready to be restored!" "But how on earth?" I asked. "Madam, I judged that it would be more pleasing for you to take the parasol along with yourself than to trust to its being brought by the other gentleman; so I just galloped my horses, overtook the coach as it was leaving this court, reclaimed the parasol, and have waited here, knowing you could take no other road to Sherborne, for the happiness of presenting it to you!" — To an ostler — "Bring the parasol!"

It was brought, and handed to me. And then I found myself making a speech in the same style, caught by the infection of the thing. I said: "Sir, this day has been full of mischances for me, but I regard the recovery of my parasol so unexpectedly as a good omen, and have a confidence that I shall now reach my destination in safety. Accept my thanks, though it is impossible to give any adequate expression to my sense of your courtesy!" I never certainly made so long and formal a speech in my life. And how I came to make it anything like it I can't imagine, unless it were under mesmerism! We bowed to each other like first cousins of Sir Charles Grandison, and I pirred on. "Do you know that gentleman?" I asked my driver. "Never saw him before."

I found Sherborne House without difficulty; and a stately, beautiful house it was, and a kind welcome it had for me. The mistake had been discovered in the morning, and great anxiety felt all day as to my fate. I was wonderfully little tired, and able to make them all (her too) laugh with my adventures. But I must positively interrupt this penny-a-lining, and go to bed. It is true to the letter, all I have told.

My two days at Sherborne House were as happy as could possibly be with that fearfully emaciated, dying woman before my eyes. They were all doing their best to be cheerful — herself as cheerful as the others. She never spoke of her death, except in taking leave of me; when she took my head in her hand and kissed it, and gave me her solemn blessing, and asked me to come again with you, to see William and the children, when she should be gone. That was a dreadful trial of my composure. I am so glad I went, it pleased her and all of them so much!

The journey back by Dorchester went all right, and

was less expensive, for I came by the second-class, and so saved the nine shillings my gig had cost me. It was a weary long way, however, from a quarter before nine till half after seven flying along in one shape or other, with only ten minutes' delay (at Southampton). My only adventure on the road back was falling in with a young unfortunate female in the Chelsea boat, the strangest compound of angel and devil I ever set eyes on, and whom, had I been a great, rich lady, I should decidedly have — brought home to tea with me and tried "to *save*." The helpless thought that I had nothing to offer her instead alone prevented me. I could not leave her however without speaking to her, and my words were so moving, through my own emotion, that she rushed from me in tears to the other side of the vessel. You may feel a certain curiosity to know what I said. I only recollect something about "her mother, alive or dead, and her evident superiority to the life she was leading." She said, "Do you think so, ma'am?" with a look of bitter wretchedness and forced gaiety that I shall never forget. She was trying to smile defiantly, when she burst into tears and ran away.

I made a frantic appeal to the workmen the other day, since when we have been getting on a little more briskly. The spokesman of them, a dashing young man, whom you have not seen, answered me: "My dear (!) madam, you must have patience, indeed you must; it will be all done — some day!" The weather is most lovely. *Monsieur le Thermomètre* pretty generally at 70°.

My health continues wonderfully good. To-day I dine at the Brookfield's, for what poor Helen used to call "a fine change." — Ever yours affectionately,

JANE W. C.

VII

Notes of a Sitter-Still

July 11, 1858

BOTKIN (what a name!), your Russian translator, has called. Luckily Charlotte had been forewarned to admit him if he came again. He is quite a different type from Tourgueneff, though a tall one, this one too. I should say he must be a Cossack — not that I ever saw a Cossack or heard one described, instinct is all I have for it. He has flattened high-boned cheeks — a nose flattened towards the point — small, very black, deep-set eyes, with thin semi-circular eyebrows — a wide thin mouth — a complexion whity-grey, and the skin of his face looked thick enough to make a saddle of! He does not possess himself like Tourgueneff, but bends and gesticulates like a Frenchman.

He burst into the room with wild expressions of his "admiration for Mr. Carlyle." I begged him to be seated, and he declared "Mr. Carlyle was the man for Russia." I tried again and again to "enchain" a rational conversation, but nothing could I get out of him but rhapsodies about you in the frightfullest English that I ever heard out of a human head! It is to be hoped that (as he told me) he reads English much better than he speaks it, else he must have produced an inconceivable translation of "Hero Worship." Such as it is, anyhow, "a large deputation of the students of St. Petersburg" waited on him (Botkin), to thank him in the strongest terms for having translated for them "Hero Worship," and made known to them Carlyle. And even the young Russian ladies now read "Hero Worship" and "unnerstants it thor-lie." He was all in a perspiration when he went away and so was I!

I should like to have asked him some questions; for example, how he came to know of your works (he had told me he had to send to England for them "at extreem cost"), but it would have been like asking a cascade! The best that I could do for him I did. I gave him a photograph of you, and put him up to carrying it in the top of his hat!

I don't think I ever told you the surprising visit I had from David Aitken [1] and Bess. I was so ill when I wrote after that all details were omitted. Charlotte had come to say one of the latch-keys was refusing to act. I went to see what the matter was, and when we opened the door, behold, David at the bottom of the steps, and Bess preparing to knock! "Is this Mrs. Carlyle's?" she asked of myself, while I was gazing dumbfoundered. "My goodness!" cried I. At the sound of my voice she knew me — not till then — though at my own door! and certainly the recognition was the furthest from complimentary I ever met. She absolutely staggered, screaming out, "God preserve me, Jane! That you?" Pleasant! David coming up the steps brought a little calm into the business, and the call got itself transacted better or worse.

They were on their way home from Italy. Both seemed rather more human than last time, especially David, whose face had taken an expression of "Peace on earth and goodwill unto men." Bess had lost a tooth or two, was rather thinner, and her eyes hollower; otherwise much the same.

[1] Minister of Minto and wife (once Bess Stoddart), Bradfute's niece and heiress.

They invited me very kindly to Minto, and he seemed really in earnest.

July 16

SURELY, dear, the shortest, most unimportant note you can write is worth a bit of paper all to itself? Such a mixed MS., with flaps too, may be a valuable literary curiosity "a hundred years hence," but it is a trial of patience to the present reader, who, on eagerly opening a letter from you, had not calculated on having to go through a process like seeking the source of the Niger, in a small way.

For the rest, you don't at all estimate my difficulties in writing a letter every day, when I am expected to tell how I am, and when "I's ashamed to say I's no better." Dispense me from saying anything whatever about my health; let me write always "Notes" and it would be easy for me to send you a daily letter. As easy at least as it is to be lively with the callers, who go away in doubt (like George Cooke) "whether I am the most stoical of women, or whether there is nothing in the world the matter with me?"

But you want to be told how I sleep, &c. &c.; and can't you understand that having said twice, thrice, call it four times, "I am sleeping hardly any, I am very nervous and suffering" the fifth time that I have the same account to repeat, "horrible is the thought to me," and I take refuge in silence. Wouldn't you do the same? Suppose, instead of putting myself in the omnibus the other day, and letting myself be carried in unbroken silence to Richmond and back again, I had sat at home writing to you all the thoughts that were in my head? But that I never would have done; not a hundredth part of the thoughts in my head have ever been or ever will be spoken or written — as long as I keep my senses, at least.

Only don't you, "the apostle of silence," find fault with me for putting your doctrine in practice. There are days when I must hold my peace or speak things all from the lips outwards, or things that, being of the nature of self-lamentation, had better never be spoken.

My cold in the meanwhile? It is still carrying on, till Lonsdale coom,[1] in the shape of cough and a stuffed head; but it does not hurt me anywhere, and I no longer need to keep to the house; the weather being warm enough, I ride in an omnibus every day more or less.

All last night it thundered; and there was one such clap as I never heard in my life, preceded by a flash that covered my book for a moment with blue light (I was reading in bed about three in the morning, and you can't think what a wild effect that blue light on the book had!). To-day it is still thundering in the distance, and soft, large, hot drops of rain falling. What of the three tailors?

I could swear you never heard of Madame —— de ——. But she has heard of you; and if you were in the habit of thanking God "for the blessing made to fly over your head," you might offer a modest thanksgiving for the honour that stunning lady did you in galloping madly all round Hyde Park in chase of your "brown wide-awake" the last day you rode there; no mortal could predict what the result would be if she came up with you. To seize your bridle and look at you till she was satisfied was a trifle to what she was supposed capable of. She only took to galloping after you when more legitimate means had failed.

She circulates everywhere, this madcap "French-

[1] Cumberland old woman.

woman." She met "the Rev. John" (Barlow), and said, when he was offering delicate attentions, "There is just one thing I wish you to do for me — to take me to see Mr. Carlyle." "Tell me to ask the Archbishop of Canterbury to dance a polka with you," said Barlow, aghast, and "I would dare it, though I have not the honour of his acquaintance; but take anybody to Mr. Carlyle — impossible!" "That silly old Barlow won't take me to Carlyle," said the lady to George Cooke; "you must do it then." "Gracious heavens!" said George Cooke; "ask me to take you up to the Queen, and introduce you to her, and I would do it, and 'take the six months' imprisonment,' or whatever punishment was awarded me; but take anybody to Mr. Carlyle — impossible!"

Soon after this, George Cooke met her riding in the Park, and said, "I passed Mr. Carlyle a little way on, in his 'brown wide-awake.'" The lady lashed her horse and set off in pursuit, leaving her party out of sight, and went all round the Park at full gallop looking out for the wide-awake. She is an authoress in a small way, this charming Frenchwoman; and is the wife of a newspaper editor at Paris, who "went into the country" (Miss F. told me) "and brought back a flowerpot full of earth, and, on the strength of that, put de —— to his name of Monsieur ——."

But the absurdest fact about her is, that, being a "Frenchwoman," she is the reputed daughter of Lord F. and a Mrs. G.! It is in Lord F.'s house that she stays here. Miss F. also declares she was a celebrated singer at Munich. But Miss F. is a very loose talker, and was evidently jealous of the sensation the lady produced by her wit and eccentricities.

Will that suit you?

XIII

THE WITTY CANON

The Rev. Sydney Smith to Lady Holland

(Extracts)

December 9, 1807

WAR, my dear Lady Holland, is natural to women, as well as men — at least with their own sex! A dreadful controversy has broken out in Bath, whether tea is most effectually sweetened by lump or pounded sugar; and the worst passions of the human mind are called into action by the pulverists and the lumpists. I have been pressed by ladies on both sides to speak in favour of their respective theories, at the Royal Institution, which I have promised to do.

September 9, 1808

I TAKE the liberty to send you two brace of grouse, — curious, because killed by a Scotch metaphysician; in other and better language, they are mere ideas, shot by other ideas, out of a pure intellectual notion, called a gun.

October 8, 1808

MY lot is now fixed and my heritage fixed, — most probably. But you may choose to make me a bishop, and if you do, I think I shall never do you discredit; for I believe it is out of the power of lawn and velvet, and the crisp hair of dead men fashioned into a wig, to make me a dishonest man; but if you do not, I am perfectly content.

June 24, 1809

I HAVE laid down two rules for the country: first, not to smite the partridge; for if I fed the poor, and comforted the sick, and instructed the ignorant, yet I should be nothing worth, if I smote the partridge. If anything ever endangers the Church, it will be the strong propensity to shooting for which the clergy are remarkable. Ten thousand good shots dispersed over the country do more harm to the cause of religion than the arguments of Voltaire and Rousseau. The squire never reads, but is it possible he can believe *that* religion to be genuine whose ministers destroy his game? . . .

Mrs. Sydney is all rural bustle, impatient for the parturition of hens and pigs; I wait patiently, knowing all will come in due season!

September 9, 1809

I DARE say it cost you much to part with Charles; but in the present state of the world, it is better to bring up our young ones to war than to peace. I burn gunpowder every day under the nostrils of my little boy, and talk to him often of fighting, to put him out of conceit with civil sciences, and prepare him for the evil times which are coming!

December 8, 1809

I HAVE been long intending to write you a letter of congratulation. There is more happiness in a multitude of children than safety in a multitude of counsellors; and if I were a rich man, I should like to have twenty children. . . .

I hear you have a good tutor for Henry, which I am exceedingly glad of. Lord Grey has met with no tutor as yet; tutors do not like to go beyond Adrian's Wall. You are aware that it is necessary to fumigate Scotch tutors: they are excellent men, but require this little preliminary caution. They are apt also to break the church windows, and get behind a hedge and fling stones at the clergyman of the parish, and betray other little symptoms of irreligion; but these you must not mind. Send me word if he has any tricks of this kind. I have seen droves of them, and know how to manage them.

1809

I MEAN to make some maxims, like Rochefoucauld, and to preserve them. My first is this: — After having lived half their lives respectable, many men get tired of honesty, and many women of propriety.

January 27, 1810

I CANNOT say how much I like the said Earl [Grey]; — a fine nature, a just and vigorous understanding, a sensitive disposition, and infirm health. These are his leading traits. His excellencies are courage, discretion, and practical sense; his deficiency, a want of executive coarseness.

November 3, 1810

WE liked Mrs. ——. It was wrong, at her time of life, to be circumvented by ——'s diagrams; but there is some excuse in the novelty of the attack, as I believe she is the first lady that ever fell a victim to algebra, or that was geometrically led from the paths of discretion.

May 23, 1811

HOW very odd, dear Lady Holland, to ask me to dine with you on Sunday, the 9th, when I am coming to stay with you from the 5th to the 12th! It is like giving a gentleman an assignation for Wednesday, when you are going to marry him on the preceding Sunday, — an attempt to combine the stimulus of gallantry with the security of connubial relations. I do not propose to be guilty of the slighest infidelity to you while I am at Holland House, except you dine in town; and then it will not be infidelity, but spirited recrimination.

September 17, 1813

FEW events are of so little consequence as the fecundity of a clergyman's wife; still your kind dispositions towards me justify me in letting you know that Mrs. Sydney and her new-born son are both extremely well. His name will be Grafton, and I shall bring him up a Methodist and a Tory.

June 25, 1814

I LIKED London better than ever I liked it before, and simply, I believe, from water-drinking. Without this, London is stupefaction and inflammation. It is not the love of wine, but thoughtlessness and unconscious imitation: other men poke out their hands for the revolving wine, and one does the same, without thinking of it. All people above the condition of labourers are ruined by excess of stimulus and nourishment, clergy included. I never yet saw any gentleman who ate and drank as little as was reasonable.

1815

NOW pray do settle in England, and remain quiet; depend upon it, it is the most agreeable place. I have heard five hundred travelled people assert that there is no such agreeable house in Europe as Holland House: why should you be the last person to be convinced of this, and the first to make it true?

February 2, 1816

MY sister was a most amiable and enlightened woman; she had run through all the stamina of constitution nature had allotted her, and died of old age, in youth. The loss of a person whom I would have cultivated as a friend, if nature had not given her to me as a relation, is a serious evil.

July 31, 1817

IT is very curious to consider in what manner Horner gained, in so extraordinary a degree, the affections of such a number of persons of both sexes, — all ages, parties, and ranks in society; for he was not remarkably good-tempered, nor particularly lively and agreeable; and an inflexible politician on the unpopular side. The causes are, his high character for probity, honour, and talents; his fine countenance; the benevolent interest he took in the concerns of all his friends; his simple and gentlemanlike manners; his untimely death.

October 1, 1823

I WAS prepared to set off for London, when a better account arrived from Dr. Bond. I think you mistake Bond's character in supposing he could be influenced by partridges. He is a man of very independent mind, with whom pheasants at least, or perhaps turkeys, are necessary.

. . . .

Nothing can be more disgusting than an Oratorio. How absurd, to see five hundred people fiddling like madmen about the Israelites in the Red Sea! Lord Morpeth pretends to say he was pleased, but I see a great change in him since the music-meeting. Pray tell Luttrell he did wrong not to come to the music. It tired me to death; it would have pleased him. He is a melodious person, and much given to sacred music. In his fits of absence I have heard him hum the Hundredth Psalm! (Old Version).

October 19, 1823

THE Duchess wrote me a very amusing note in answer to mine, for which I am much obliged. All duchesses seem agreeable to clergymen; but she would really be a very clever, agreeable woman, if she were married to a neighbouring vicar; and I should often call upon her.

November 6, 1827

JEFFREY has been here with his adjectives, who always travel with him. His throat is giving way; so much wine goes down it, so many million words leap over it, how can it rest? Pray make him a judge; he is a truly great man, and is very heedless of his own interests. I lectured him on his romantic folly of wishing his friends to be preferred before himself, and succeeded, I think, in making him a little more selfish.

BRISTOL, *February* 17, 1828

AN extremely comfortable prebendal house; seven-stall stables and room for four carriages, so that I can hold all your *cortège* when you come; looks to the south, and is perfectly snug and parsonic; masts of West-Indiamen seen from the windows. The colleagues I have found here are a Mr. Ridley, cousin to Sir Matthew; a very good-natured, agreeable man, — deaf, tottering, worldly-minded, vain as a lawyer, noisy, and perfectly good-natured and obliging. The little Dean I have not seen; he is as small as the Bishop, they say. It is supposed that the one of these ecclesiastics elevated upon the shoulders of the other, would fall short of the Archbishop of Canterbury's wig. The Archbishop of York is forced to go down on his knees to converse with the Bishop of Bristol, just as an elephant kneels to receive its rider.

December 14, 1829

I TOLD —— if he would have patience he would have a little girl at last. I might have said, he might have twenty little girls. What is there to prevent him from having a family sufficient to exasperate the placid Malthus?

Luttrell came over for a day, from whence I know not, but I thought not from good pastures; at least, he had not his usual soup-and-pattie look. There was a forced smile upon his countenance, which seemed to indicate plain roast and boiled, and a sort of apple-pudding depression, as if he had been staying with a clergyman.

May 1831

I MET John Russell at Exeter. The people along the road were very much disappointed by his smallness.

I told them he was much larger before the Bill was thrown out, but was reduced by excessive anxiety about the people. This brought tears into their eyes!

July 1831

PHILOSOPHER MALTHUS came here last week. I got an agreeable party for him of unmarried people. There was only one lady who had had a child; but he is a good-natured man, and, if there are no appearances of approaching fertility, is civil to every lady. Malthus is a real moral philosopher, and I would almost consent to speak as inarticulately, if I could think and act as wisely.

I sit in my beautiful study, looking upon a thousand flowers, and read agreeable books, in order to keep up arguments with Lord Holland and Allen. I thank God heartily for my comfortable situation in my old age, — above my deserts, and beyond my former hopes.

ABBEVILLE, *October* 2, 1835

THERE is a family of English people living here who have been here for five years. They stopped to change horses, liked the place, and have been here ever since: father, mother, two handsome daughters, and some young children. I should think it not unlikely that one of the daughters will make a nuptial alliance with the waiter, or give her hand to the son of the landlord, in order to pay the bill. . . .

We are well, and are going to sit down to a dinner at five francs a-head. We are going regularly through the Burgundy wines, — the most pernicious, and of course the best: Macon the first day, Chablis the second — both excellent; to-day Volnay.

June 1840

I AM giving a rout this evening to the only three persons I have yet discovered at Brighton. I have had handbills printed to find other London people, but I believe there are none. I shall stay till the 28th. You *must* allow the Chain Pier to be a great luxury; and I think all rich and rational people living in London should take small doses of Brighton from time to time. There cannot be a better place than this to refresh metropolitan gentlemen and ladies, wearied with bad air, falsehood, and lemonade.

November 6, 1842

I HAVE not the heart, when an amiable lady says, "Come to 'Semiramis' in my box," to decline; but I got bolder at a distance. "Semiramis" would be to me pure misery. I love music very little, — I hate acting; I have the worst opinion of Semiramis herself, and the whole thing (I cannot help it) seems so childish and so foolish that I cannot abide it. Moreover, it would be rather out of etiquette for a Canon of St. Paul's to go to an opera; and where etiquette prevents me from doing things disagreeable to myself, I am a perfect martinet.

All these things considered, I am sure you will not be a Semiramis to me, but let me off.

XIV

CHARACTERS

Mr. Gabriel Bullock offers his heart to Mrs. Margaret Clark

(To her I very much respect, Mrs. Margaret Clark)

LOVELY, and oh that I could write loving Mrs. Margaret Clark, I pray you let Affection excuse Presumption. Having been so happy as to enjoy the Sight of your sweet Countenance and comely Body, sometimes when I had occasion to buy Treacle or Liquorish Power at the apothecary's shop, I am so enamoured with you, that I can no more keep close my flaming Desire to become your Servant. And I am the more bold now to write to your sweet self, because I am now my own Man, and may match were I please; for my Father is taken away; and now I am come to my Living, which is ten yard Land, and a House; and there is never a Yard Land in our Field but is as well worth ten Pound a Year as a Thief's worth a Halter; and all my Brothers and Sisters are provided for: besides I have good Household Stuff, though I say it, both Brass and Pewter, Linnens and Woollens; and though my House be thatched, yet if you and I match, it shall go hard but I will have one half of it slated. If you shall think well of this Motion, I will wait upon you as soon as my new Cloaths is made, and Hay-Harvest is in. I could, though I say it, have good Matches in our Town; but my Mother (God's Peace be with her) charged me upon her Death-Bed to marry a Gentlewoman, one who had been well trained up in Sowing and Cookery. I do not think but that if you and I can agree to marry, and lay our Means together, I shall be made grand Jury-man e'er two or three Years come about, and that will be a great Credit to us. If I could have got a Messenger for Sixpence, I would have sent one on Purpose, and some Trifle or other for a Token of my Love; but I hope there is nothing lost for that neither. So hoping you will take this Letter in good Part, and answer it with what Care and Speed you can, I rest and remain,

Yours, if my own, MR. GABRIEL BULLOCK,
now my father is dead.

SWEPSTON, LEICESTERSHIRE

When the Coal Carts come, I shall send oftener; and may come in one of them myself.

Sir John Dalrymple details his ill-luck

(To Admiral Dalrymple)

CRANSTON, *January* 1, 1772

MY DEAR SIR.—Your shirts are safe. I have made many attempts upon them; but Bess, who has in honesty what she wants in temper, keeps them in safety for you.

The Second Post

You ask me what I have been doing? To the best of my memory, what has passed since I came home is as follows.

Finding the roof bad, I sent slaters, at the peril of their necks, to repair it. They mended three holes, and made thirty themselves.

I pulled down as many walls round the house as would have fortified a town. This was in summer: but now that winter is come, I would give all the money to put them up again, that it cost me to take them down.

I thought it would give a magnificent air to the old hall, to throw the passage into it. After it was done, I went out of town to see how it looked. It was night when I went into it; the wind blew out the candle from the over-size of the room; upon which, I ordered the partition to be built up again, that I might not die of cold in the midst of summer.

I ordered the old timber to be thinned; to which, perhaps, the love of lucre a little contributed. The workmen, for every tree they cut, destroyed three, by letting them fall on each other. I received a momentary satisfaction from hearing that the carpenter I employed had cut off his thumb in felling a tree. But this pleasure was soon allayed, when, upon examining his measure, I found that he had measured false, and cheated me of 20 *per cent*.

Instead of saddle-horses I bought mares, and had them covered with an Arabian. When I went, some months after, to mount them, the groom told me, I should kill the foals; and now I walk on foot, with the stable full of horses, unless when, with much humility, I ask to be admitted into the chaise, which is generally refused me.

Remembering, with a pleasing complacency, the

Watcombe pigs, I paid thirty shillings for a sow with pig. My wife starved them. They ran over to a madman, called Lord Adam Gordon, who distrained them for damage; and the mother, with ten helpless infants, died of bad usage.

Loving butter much, and cream more, I bought two Dutch cows, and had plenty of both. I made my wife a present of two more: she learned the way to market for their produce; and I have never got a bowl of cream since.

I made a fine hay-stack; but quarreled with my wife as to the manner of drying the hay, and building the stack. The hay-stack took fire; by which I had the double mortification of losing my hay, and finding my wife had more sense than myself.

I kept no plough; for which I thank my Maker; because then I must have wrote this Letter from a gaol.

I paid twenty pounds for a dunghill, because I was told it was a good thing; and, now, I would give any body twenty shillings to tell me what to do with it.

I built, and stocked a pigeon-house; but the cats watched below, the hawks hovered above; and pigeon-soup, roasted pigeon, or cold pigeon-pie, have I never seen since.

I fell to drain a piece of low ground behind the house; but I hit upon the tail of the rock, and drained the well of the house; by which I can get no water for my victuals.

I entered into a great project for selling lime, upon a promise from one of my own farmers to give me land off his farm. But when I went to take off the ground, he laughed, said he had choused the Lawyer, and exposed me to a dozen law-suits for breach of bargains, which I could not perform.

I fattened black cattle and sheep; but could not agree with the butchers about the price. From mere economy, we ate them ourselves, and almost killed all the family with surfeits.

I bought two score of six-year old wethers for my own table; but a butcher, who rented one of the fields, put my mark upon his own carrion sheep; by which I have been living upon carrion all the summer.

I brewed much beer; but the small turned sour, and the servants drank all the strong.

I found a ghost in the house, whose name was M'Alister, a pedlar, that had been killed in one of the rooms at the top of the house two centuries ago. No servant would go on an errand after the sun was set, for fear of M'Alister, which obliged me to send off one set of my servants. Soon after the housekeeper, your old friend Mrs. Brown, died, aged 90; and then the belief ran, that another ghost was in the house, upon which many of the new set of servants begged leave to quit the house, and got it.

In one thing only I have succeeded. I have quarreled with all my neighbours; so that, with a dozen gentlemen's seats in my view, I stalk alone like a lion in a desart.

I thought I should have been happy with my tenants, because I could be insolent to them without their being insolent to me. But they paid me no rent; and in a few days I shall have above one half of the very few friends I have in the country in a prison.

Such being the pleasures of a country life, I intend to quit them all in about a month, to submit to the mortification of spending the spring in London, where, I am happy to hear, we are to meet. But I am infinitely happier to hear that Mrs. Dalrymple is doing so well.

May God preserve her long to you! for she is a fine creature.

Just when I was going to you last spring, I received a Letter from Bess, that she was dying. I put off my journey to Watcombe, and almost killed myself with posting to Scotland, where I found Madam in perfect good health. — Yours always, my dear Jack,

JOHN DALRYMPLE

Sir Hew Dalrymple recommends Dishington for preferment

(To Sir Lawrence Dundas)

WALZELL, *May* 24, 1775

DEAR SIR, — Having spent a long life in pursuit of pleasure and health, I am now retired from the world in poverty and with the gout; so, joining with Solomon, that, "all is vanity and vexation of spirit," I go to church and say my prayers.

I assure you that most of us religious people reap some little satisfaction, in hoping that you wealthy voluptuaries have a fair chance of being damned to all eternity; and that Dives shall call out for a drop of water to Lazarus, one drop of which he seldom tasted when he had the twelve Apostles in his cellar.[1]

Now, sir, that doctrine being laid down, I wish to give you, my friend, a loophole to creep through. Going to church last Sunday, as usual, I saw an unknown face in the pulpit, and rising up to prayers, as others do upon like occasions, I began to look round the church to see

[1] Twelve hogsheads of claret.

if there were any pretty girls there, when my attention was attracted by the foreign accent of the parson. I gave him my attention, and had my devotion awakened by the most pathetic prayer I ever heard. This made me all attention to the sermon; a finer discourse never came from the lips of a man. I returned in the afternoon, and heard the same preacher exceed his morning work by the finest chain of reasoning, conveyed by the most eloquent expressions. I immediately thought of what Agrippa said to Paul, "Almost thou persuadest me to be a Christian." I sent to ask the man of God to honour my roof and dine with me. I asked him of his country, and what not; I even asked him if his sermons were his own composition, which he affirmed they were; I assured him I believed it, for never man had spoke or wrote so well. "My name is Dishington," said he. "I am an assistant to an old minister in the Orkneys, who enjoys a fruitful benefice of £50 a year, out of which I am allowed £20 for preaching and instructing 1,200 people who live in two separate Islands; out of which I pay £1,5s. to the boatman to transport me from the one to the other. I should be happy could I continue in that terrestrial paradise; but we have a great Lord who has many little people soliciting him for many little things that he can do and that he cannot do; and if my minister dies, his succession is too great a prize not to raise up many powerful rivals to baulk my hope of preferment."

I asked him if he possessed any other wealth. "Yes," said he, "I married the prettiest girl in the island; she has blessed me with three children, and as we are both young, we may expect more. Besides, I am so beloved in the island, that I have all my peats brought home carriage free."

This is my story, — now to the prayer of my petition. I never before envied you the possession of the Orkneys, which I now do only to provide for this eloquent innocent apostle.

The sun has refused your barren isles his kindly influence; do not deprive them of so pleasant a preacher; let not so great a treasure be forever lost to the damned inhospitable country; for, I assure you, were the Archbishop of Canterbury to hear him, or hear of him, he would not do less than make him an archdeacon. The man has but one weakness, that of preferring the Orkneys to all the earth.

This way, and no other, you have a chance for Salvation. Do this man good, and he will pray for you. This will be a better purchase than your Irish Estate, or the Orkneys. I think it will help me forward too, since I am the man who told you of the man so worthy and deserving; so pious, so eloquent, and whose prayers may do so much good. — Till I hear from you on this head, yours, in all meekness, love and benevolence.

H. D.

P.S. — Think what an unspeakable pleasure it will be, to look down from Heaven, and see Rigby, Masterton, all the Campbells and nabobs, swimming in fire and brimstone, while you are sitting with Whitefield and his old women, looking beautiful, frisking and singing; all which you may have by settling this man, after the death of the present incumbent.

A Welsh gentleman obtains a situation for his son in the East India House

(To the Honourable Board of Directors of the East India Co.)

GENTLEMEN, — I have a parcel of fine boys, but not much cash to provide for them. I had intended my eldest son for the Church, but I find he is more likely to kick a church down than support it. I sent him to the University, but he could not submit himself to the college rules, and, on being reproved by his tutors, he took it up in the light of an affair of honour, and threatened to call them to account for it. All my plans for his welfare being thus disconcerted, I asked him if he had formed any for himself; he replied, he meant to go to India. I then inquired if he had any interest, at which question he looked somewhat foolish, and replied in the negative. Now, gentlemen, I know no more of you than you do of me. I therefore may appear to you not much wiser than my son. I can only say that he is of Welsh extraction for many generations, and, as my first-born, I flatter myself, has not degenerated. He is six feet high, of an athletic make, and bold and intrepid as a lion. If you like to see him I will equip him as a gentleman, and, I am, Gentlemen, etc.

Shelley (at school) prepares a firm of publishers for the worst

(To Longman & Co.)

Eton College, *May* 7, 1809

GENTLEMEN, — It is my intention to complete and publish a Romance, of which I have already written a large portion, before the end of July. My object in writing it was not pecuniary, as I am independent, being the heir of a gentleman of large fortune in the county of Sussex, and prosecuting my studies as an Oppidan at Eton; from the many leisure hours I have, I have taken an opportunity of indulging my favourite propensity in writing. Should it produce any pecuniary advantages, so much the better for me, I do not expect it. If you would be so kind as to answer this, direct it to me at the Rev. George Bethell's. Might I likewise request the favour of secrecy until the Romance is published. — I am, your very humble servant, Percy Shelley

Be so good as to tell me whether I shall send you the original manuscript when I have completed it or one corrected, etc.

Charles Dickens introduces Professor Felton to the great Dando

London, *July* 31, 1842

MY DEAR FELTON, — Of all the monstrous and incalculable amount of occupation that ever beset one unfortunate man, mine has been the most stupendous since I came home. The dinners I have had to eat, the places I have had to go to, the letters I have had to answer, the sea of business and of pleasure in which I have been plunged, not even the genius of an —— or the pen of a —— could describe.

Wherefore I indite a monstrously short and wildly uninteresting epistle to the American Dando; but perhaps you don't know who Dando was. He was an oyster-eater, my dear Felton. He used to go into oyster-shops, without a farthing of money, and stand at the counter eating natives, until the man who opened them grew pale, cast down his knife, staggered backward, struck his white forehead with his open hand, and cried, "You are Dando!!!" He has been known to eat twenty dozen at one sitting, and would have eaten forty, if the truth had not flashed upon the shopkeeper. For these offences he was constantly committed to the House of Correction. During his last imprisonment he was taken ill, got worse and worse, and at last began knocking violent double knocks at Death's door. The doctor stood beside his bed, with his fingers on his pulse. "He is going," says the doctor. "I see it in his eye. There is only one thing that would keep life in him for another hour, and that is — oysters." They were immediately brought. Dando swallowed eight, and feebly took a ninth. He held it in his mouth and looked round the bed strangely. "Not a bad one, is it?" says the doctor. The patient shook his head, rubbed his trembling hand upon his stomach, bolted the oyster, and fell back — dead. They buried him in the prison yard, and paved his grave with oyster shells.

We are all well and hearty, and have already begun to wonder what time next year you and Mrs. Felton and Dr. Howe will come across the briny sea together. To-morrow we go to the seaside for two months. I am looking out for news of Longfellow, and shall be delighted when I know that he is on his way to London and this house.

I am bent upon striking at the piratical newspapers with the sharpest edge I can put upon my small axe, and hope in the next session of Parliament to stop their entrance into Canada. For the first time within the memory of man, the professors of English literature seem disposed to act together on this question. It is a good thing to aggravate a scoundrel, if one can do nothing else, and I think *we* can make them smart a little in this way. . . .

I wish you had been at Greenwich the other day, where a party of friends gave me a private dinner; public ones I have refused. C—— was perfectly wild at the reunion, and, after singing all manner of marine songs, wound up the entertainment by coming home (six miles) in a little open phaeton of mine, *on his head*, to the mingled delight and indignation of the metropolitan police. We were very jovial indeed; and I assure you that I drank your health with fearful vigour and energy.

On board that ship coming home I established a club, called the United Vagabonds, to the large amusement of the rest of the passengers. This holy brotherhood committed all kinds of absurdities, and dined always, with a variety of solemn forms, at one end of the table, below the mast, away from all the rest. The captain being ill when we were three or four days out, I produced my medicine chest and recovered him. We had a few more sick men after that, and I went round "the wards" every day in great state, accompanied by two Vagabonds, habited as Ben Allen and Bob Sawyer, bearing enormous rolls of plaster and huge pairs of scissors. We were really very merry all the way, breakfasted in one party at Liverpool, shook hands, and parted most cordially. . . . — Affectionately your faithful Friend.

P.S. — I have looked over my journal, and have decided to produce my American trip in two volumes. I have written about half the first since I came home, and hope to be out in October. This is "exclusive news," to be communicated to any friends to whom you may like to intrust it, my dear F.

XV

THE OLD LION

W. S. Landor: extracts from his correspondence

(To Southey)

1810

IN architects I have passed from a great scoundrel to a greater, a thing I thought impossible; and have been a whole year in making a farmhouse habitable. It is not half finished, and has cost already two thousand pounds. I think seriously of filling it with chips and straw, and setting fire to it. Never was anything half so ugly, though there is not a brick or tile throughout. Again and again I lament I was disappointed in my attempt to fix in your delightful country. The earth contains no race of human beings so totally vile and worthless as the Welsh. . . . I have expended in labour, within three years, eight thousand pounds amongst them, and yet they treat me as their greatest enemy. . . . When I had the happiness of meeting you in Bristol, you mentioned your design of coming into Monmouthshire this summer. I hope nothing will hinder it. Before two months have passed, I can give you a comfortable bed. I have two small rooms finished, and my kitchen will be completed in six weeks.

1811

JEFFREY is called a clever man, I hear. If so, people may be clever men without knowing the nature of a lie, or the distinction between virtue and vice. No species of dishonesty is surely so unpardonable as Jeffrey's, no profligacy so flagitious. Thievery may arise from early example or from urgent want. It may have grown into an incurable habit, or have been pushed on by the necessities of nature. A man may commit even murder itself from the sudden and incontrollable impulse of a heart still uncorrupted; but he must possess one of a very different kind who can air and exercise his faculties on no other ground than the destruction of fame and the mortification of genius. I was once asked whether I would be introduced to this gentleman. My reply was, No, nor to any other rascal whatsoever. I like to speak plainly, and particularly so when the person of whom I speak may profit by it.

1814

EVERY hope of meeting you again in England has vanished. Pardon me if this is only the second of my wishes. My first is, that I may become by degrees indifferent to this country. The Court of Exchequer has decided in my favour; but B has been able to promise bail and a replevy, so that the ends of justice are defeated. Nearly three years' rent will be due before I can receive one farthing from him; and all my timber is spoiled. I shall be utterly ruined. Not being able to pay the interest of 10,000*l.* debt on the Llanthony estate, the mortgagee will instantly seize on it until he has paid himself the whole of the principal. The laws of England are made entirely for the protection of guilt. A creditor could imprison me for twenty pounds, while a man who owes me two thousand, and keeps me from the possession of two thousand more, can convert wealth and affluence into poverty and distress, — can, in short, drive me for ever from my native country, and riot with impunity on the ruins of my estate. I had promised my mother to visit her. I never can hope to see her again. She is seventy-two, and her sorrow at my overwhelming and most unmerited misfortunes will too surely shorten her days. My wife, when she married, little thought she should leave all her friends to live in obscurity and perhaps in want. For my sake she refused one of the largest fortunes that any private gentleman possesses, and another person of distinguished rank. Whoever comes near me is either unhappy or ungrateful. There is no act of forbearance or of kindness which B did not receive from me. His father saw and knew perfectly that his farming must ruin him. Yet, instead of persuading him to resign it, he sent the remainder of his family to live with him, and to countenance him in all his violence and roguery. I go to-morrow to St. Malo. In what part of France I shall end my days, I know not, but there I shall end them; and God grant that I may end them speedily, and so as to leave as little sorrow as possible to my friends. No time will alter my regard and veneration for you; nor shall anything lessen the kind sentiments you entertain for me. It is a great privilege to hold the hearts of the virtuous. If men in general knew how great it is, could they ever consent to abandon it? I am alone here. My wife follows me when I have found a place fit for her reception. Adieu!

1825

HIS first villany in making me disappoint the person with whom I had agreed for the pictures instigated me to throw my fourth volume, in its imperfect state, into the fire, and has cost me nine-tenths of my fame as a writer. His next villany will entail perhaps a chancery-suit on my children, — for at its commencement I blow my brains out. . . . Mr. Hazlitt, Mr. Leigh Hunt, Lord Dillon, Mr. Brown, and some other authors of various kinds, have been made acquainted, one from another, with this whole affair; and they speak of it as a thing unprecedented. . . . It is well I did it [an Imaginary Conversation] before Taylor had given me a fresh proof of his intolerable roguery. This cures me forever, if I live, of writing what could be published; and I will take good care that my son shall not suffer in the same way. Not a line of any kind will I leave behind me. My children shall be carefully warned against literature. To fence, to swim, to speak French, are the most they shall learn.

(To his Sisters)

1830

BUT my country now is Italy, where I have a residence for life, and literally may sit under my own vine and my own fig-tree. I have some thousands of the one and some scores of the other, with myrtles, pomegranates, oranges, lemons, gagias, and mimosas in great quantity. I intend to make a garden not very unlike yours at Warwick; but, alas, time is wanting. I *may* live another ten years, but do not expect it. In a few days, whenever the weather will allow it, I have four mimosas ready to place round my intended tomb, and a friend who is coming to plant them.

1831

I MUST now give you a description of the place. The front of the house is towards the north, looking at the ancient town of Fiesole, three quarters of a mile off. The hills of Fiesole protect it from the north and northeast winds. The hall is 31 ft. by 22, and 20 high. On the right is a drawing-room 22 by 20; and through it you come to another 26 by 20. All are 20 ft. high. Opposite the door is another leading down to the offices on right and left; and between them to a terrace-walk about a hundred yards long, overlooking Valdarno and Vallombrosa, celebrated by Milton. On the right of the downward staircase is the upward staircase to the bed-rooms; and on the left are two other rooms corresponding with the two drawing-rooms. Over the hall, which is vaulted, is another room of equal size, delightfully cool in summer. I have four good bedrooms upstairs, 13 ft. high. One smaller and two servants' bedrooms over these, 10½ ft. high. In the centre of the house is a high turret, a dovecote. The house is 60 ft. high on the terrace side, and 50 on the other; the turret is 18 ft. above the 60. I have two gardens: one with a fountain and fine jet-d'eau. In the two are 165 large lemon-trees and 20 orange-trees, with two conservatories to keep them in, in winter. The whole could not be built in these days for 10,000*l*.

I am putting everything into good order by degrees; in fact, I spend in improvements what I used to spend in house-rent: that is about 75*l*. a year. I have planted 200 cypresses, 600 vines, 400 roses, 200 arbutuses, and 70 bays, besides laurustinas, etc. etc. and 60 fruit-trees of the best qualities from France. I have not had a moment's illness, since I resided here, nor have the children. My wife runs after colds; it would be strange if she did not take them; but she has taken none here; hers are all from Florence. I have the best water, the best air, and the best oil in the world. They speak highly of the wine too; but here I doubt. In fact, I hate wine, unless hock or claret.

LLANTHONY, I am afraid, will never be occupied by any one. I proposed to take down the house, and sell the materials; for certainly neither I nor Arnold will ever live there. I never think of it without thinking of the ruin to which it has brought me; leaving me one of the poorest Englishmen in Florence, instead of one of the richest.

(To Lady Blessington)

FLORENCE, *March* 14, 1833

A GERMAN tutor is coming to manage A[rnold], within a few days; I can hardly bring him to construe a little Greek with me, and what is worse, he is not always disposed to fence with me. I foresee he will be a worse dancer than I am if possible; in vain I tell him what is very true, that I have suffered more from my bad dancing, than from all the other misfortunes and miseries of my life put together. Not dancing well! I never danced at all; and how grievously has my heart ached when others were in the full enjoyment of that recreation, which I had no right even to partake of.

Hare has lately bought a Raffael here for four hundred

louis. It is a Raffael, indeed, but a copy from Pietro Perugino.

The original is extant, and much finer than the copy. Raffael was but a boy when he painted it; he and his master are the only two painters that ever had a perfect idea of feminine beauty.

"Raffael, when he went to Rome, lost Paradise, and had only Eden;" his Fornarina, and others, are fine women, but not such women as the first, that God made, or as the one that he chose to be the idol of half the world. Titian, less fortunate than Lawrence, was rarely employed to paint a beauty; those that he and Correggio chose for models had no grace or loveliness; Leonardo's are akin to ugliness.

FLORENCE, *July* 16, 1833

I FIND that Coleridge has lost the beneficent friend, at whose house he lived. George IV., the vilest wretch in Europe, gave him £100 a year, enough, in London, to buy three turnips and half an egg a day. Those men surely were the most dexterous of courtiers, who resolved to shew William that his brother was not the vilest, by dashing the half egg and three turnips from the plate of Coleridge. No such action as this is recorded of any administration in the British annals, and I am convinced that there is not a state in Europe, or Asia, in which the paltriest minister of the puniest despot would recommend it.

FLORENCE, *February* 15, 1834

THE book indeed is the "Book of Beauty," both inside and outside. Nevertheless, I must observe that neither here nor in any other engraving, do I find a resemblance of you. I do not find the expression. Lawrence has not succeeded either, unless you have the gift of changing it almost totally. The last change in that case was for the better — but pray stay here.

I have a little spite against the frontispiece, and am resolved to prefer Francesca. If I had seen such a person any time towards the close of the last century, I am afraid I should have been, what some rogue called me upon a very different occasion, much later, *matto! ma matto!* Age breaks down the prison in which beauty has enthralled us; but I suspect there are some of us, like the old fellow let loose from the Bastille, who would gladly get in again were it possible.

You are too generous in praising me for my admiration of Wordsworth and Southey. This is only a proof that I was not born to be a poet. I am not a good hater; I only hate pain and trouble. I think I could have hated Bonaparte if he had been a gentleman. Castlereagh was almost as mischievous, and was popularly a gentleman; but being an ignorant and weak creature, he escapes from hatred without a bruise.

The Whigs, I am afraid, are as little choice of men as the Tories are of means. It is among the few felicities of my life that I never was attached to a party or a party man. I have always excused myself from dinners, that I may never meet one.

January 13, 1835

I HAVE been reading Beckford's Travels, and Vathek. The last pleases me less than it did forty years ago, and yet the Arabian Nights have lost none of their charms for me. All the learned and wiseacres in England cried out against this wonderful work, upon its first appearance; Gray among the rest. Yet I doubt whether any man, except Shakespeare, has afforded so much delight, if we open our hearts to receive it. The author of the Arabian Nights was the greatest benefactor the East ever had, not excepting Mahomet. How many hours of pure happiness has he bestowed on six-and-twenty millions of hearers. All the springs of the desert have less refreshed the Arabs than those delightful tales, and they cast their gems and genii over our benighted and foggy regions.

B[eckford], in his second letter, says, that two or three of Rosa da Tivoli's landscapes merit observation, and in the next he scorns P. Potter. Now all Rosa da Tivoli's works are not worth a blade of grass from the hand of P. Potter. The one was a consummate artist; the other one of the coarsest that ever bedaubed a canvas. He talks of "the worst roads that ever *pretended* to be made use of," and of a *dish* of tea, without giving us the ladle or the carving knife for it. When I read such things, I rub my eyes, and awaken my recollections. I not only fancy that I am older than I am in reality (which is old enough, in all conscience), but that I have begun to lose my acquaintance with our idiom. Those who desire to write upon light matters gracefully, must read with attention the writings of Pope, Lady M. W. Montague, and Lord Chesterfield — three ladies of the first water.

I am sorry you sent my "Examination" by a private hand. I never in my life sent a note by a private hand. Nothing affects me but pain and disappointment. Hannah More says, "There are no evils in the world but sin and bile." They fall upon me very unequally. I would give a good quantity of bile for a trifle of sin, and yet my philosophy would induce me to throw it aside.

No man ever began so early to abolish hope and wishes. Happy he, who is resolved to walk with Epicurus on his right and Epictetus on his left, and to shut his ears to every other voice along the road.

March 16, 1835

AFTER a year or more, I receive your reminiscences of Byron. Never, for the love of God, send anything again by a Welshman. I mean anything literary.

1836

WORDSWORTH, no doubt, has a thousand good reasons why there is not a poet upon earth; but as there are many who have given me pleasure, I love them for it; some of them perhaps a little more than they deserve. All men are liable to error. I particularly, who believe that there may be criticism without sarcasm, and Christianity without deans and chapters.

The surface of Wordsworth's mind, the poetry, has a good deal of staple about it, and will bear handling; but the inner, the conversational and private, has many coarse intractable dangling threads, fit only for the flock-bed equipage of grooms. I praised him before I knew more of him; else I never should: and I might have been unjust to the better part had I remarked the worse sooner. This is a great fault, to which we are all liable, from an erroneous idea of consistency.

Beside, there is a little malice, I fear, at the bottom of our hearts (men's, I mean, of course).

Undated

WHEN I have once composed a thing, I never care what becomes of it. This, and being grey, are the only things in which I differ from what I was. What treasures I thought my trumpery some thirty or fourty years ago.

Do not let Count D'Orsay shoot any more little birds. I never see one fall but its ghost haunts me, and "thou canst not say I did it" is quite vain.

May 21, 1837

I HEAR they have been reviewing me in the Quarterly. I wonder where they found their telescope. By the account I receive of it, it wants nothing but glasses. How perilous it is to tread upon the heels of truth!

BATH, *January* 19, 1838

THE best, however, that ever was written, either in Latin or any other language, is attributed to Shenstone. Vale (I forget who) Heu quanto minus est cum reliquis versari, quam tui meminisse!

When will any man write anything worth this again? It never comes into my mind but it takes entire possession of my heart, and I am as incapable of reading for an hour after, as if I had just left Hamlet or Othello. There are single sentences in the world, far outvaluing three or four hundred authors, all entire; as there have been individual men out-valuing whole nations; Washington, for instance, and Kosciusko, and Hofer, were fairly worth all the other men of their times; I mean that each was.

Your friend, Lord Durham, must either be a very patriotic man, or a very ambitious one. I confess to you, my ambition and patriotism united would not induce me to undertake what he has undertaken, for the possession of all America, North and South. I am so timid and thoughtless a creature, that I would not have a chilblain for a kingdom. I would not even dip this pen in ink, if it cost me any exertion, to set obstinate fools rather more right than they were before. What are they? chaff, soon blown away, to make room for other chaff, threshed on the same floor. Superstition and fraud must be drawn out of the ring, then men will have fair play, and fight for any stake that suits them.

Undated

MR. BROWN accompanied poor Keats on a visit to W[ordsworth]. Keats read to him a part of his "Endymion," in which, I think he told me, there is a "Hymn to Pan." W—— looked red, though grave; and said, at last, "A pretty piece of paganism."

This reminds me of Kenyon's question to [Crabb] Robinson, — "Did you ever, you who have travelled with him for months together, did you ever hear him speak favourably of any author whatsoever?"

Robinson's reply was, "He certainly is not given to the laudatory."

He well deserves the flagellation I have given him, for his impudence in regard to Southey. But to make amends, if ever he writes five such things as you will find at the end of my volume, I will give him as many hundred pounds. I will now publish nothing more, for the remainder of my life.

December, 1838

PIETY is greatly on the increase at Bath, not only conceited Evangelism, but most genuine piety, and among men who certainly make no false pretentions.

The last time I was at the rooms, I heard two go through the same formula on the same occasion. They both had been waiting in the lobby, and they both had been blest by having handed their ladies into their carriages. One shuffled his shoulders, and the other dilated both nostrils, and each exclaimed with equal devotion, "Thank God!"

January 1, 1839

I HAVE this instant sent your note to poor ——. I never was paid so well for celebrity. It has made him very ill. He is now about to publish a drama on the Deluge, on which he tells me he has been engaged for twenty years. You cannot be surprised that he is grievously and hopelessly afflicted, having had water on his brain so long. The threatened deluge makes me open my prayer-book to look for the blessed words of the Royal Psalmist, and join his Majesty in "O that I were a bird!" a water bird of course, wild goose, sheldrake, gull, etc., in short, anything that might possibly escape from the interior of the ark, for which (I fear) not a drop of spirit has been provided.

January 15, 1839

I HAVE been in Berkshire for four days, on a visit to Hare, who insisted on my keeping his birthday. He is residing at West Woodhay House, built by Inigo Jones. It would do passably well for Naples, better for Timbuctoo. All but my victuals were congealed. I almost envied the bed of Procrustes, so enormous was mine, such a frozen sea. A company of comedians might have acted in it any piece they chose, and there would have been ample room for prompter and orchestra. I was ready to say my prayers when I was delivered from it.

March 7, 1839

THIS morning I have taken back to the circulating library the last volume of Vidocq. If I had time, or rather, if I took any great interest in two such people as the great thief and the great thief-taker, I would compose a parallel, inch by inch, of these two men.[1] One of them frightened all the good, the other all the bad — one betrayed all his employers, the other all his accomplices — one sacrificed the hopeful to ambition, the other the desperate to justice.

I doubt whether in seven years I could form the corollary more completely than I have done in the seventh of a minute, but it will require a century to make men honest and wise enough to bear the question "which is best?" The whole race of moral swindlers and ring-droppers must be taken up first. When God has stripped us all of furs and flounces, our just proportions will be discovered better.

BATH, *November* 17, 1839

I COULD be well content in solitude as deep as his. Never were my spirits better than in my thirtieth year, when I wrote "Gebir," and did not exchange twelve sentences with men. I lived among woods, which are now killed with copper works, and took my walk over sandy sea-coast deserts, then covered with low roses and thousands of nameless flowers and plants, trodden by the naked feet of the Welsh peasantry, and trackless.

1839(?)

DIGBY, who became a Catholic, and Padre Pagani, who probably is the next in learning to Digby among the Catholics, are inclined to convert me. Doubt-

[1] Napoleon, Vidocq.

less it is an amusement to them to throw the rod and line over the running stream: the trout laughs in his sleeves, and sidles, and shows all his specks. Alas! I can no longer sing my old version of Adeste Fideles, for want of a chorus — "Adeste Fideles! læte triumphantes!" etc.

A few months ago I went to occupy my former seat in the Catholic Chapel, where I had once been seated between Mrs. Fitzherbert and Helen Walsh Porter. On the wall, at the extremity of it, I saw a marble tablet. I went toward it, and there I found the name of my oldest friend, Mrs. Ferrers, and just beyond it was her daughter's. I will venture to say, and I do it without pride, I was at that moment the most religious and devout man in the whole chapel. It is true I did not hear the service, and the music, which was so mingled with the affections as to be lost among them: yet, instead of wishing to be reminded of soft words and tender looks, which I went for, the faces of old friends rose up from the grave before me, and were far more welcome. I waited until all were gone out, and then I placed my brow against the edge of the monument. Age has its follies, you see, no less than youth.

BATH, *December* 1, 1839

ON Wednesday last, I was present at a wedding; the only one I ever was at, excepting one other. There was bride-cake, and there were verses in profusion, two heavy commodities! But what an emblematic thing the bride-cake is! All sugar above, and all lumpiness below. But may Heaven grant another, and far different destiny, to my sweet-tempered, innocent, sensible young friend.

BATH, *April* 1, 1841

IT is beginning to rain again. What are our bishops at? But their venison never was fatter.

No date

YOU cannot doubt how proud and happy I shall be to be your guest. If you should not have left London in the beginning of May, do not be shocked at hearing that a cab is come to the door with a fierce looking old man in it.

BATH, *July* 4, 1841

I AM delighted to find how gloriously my friend Dickens has been received at Edinburgh. But the Scotchmen could not avoid ill-placed criticisms, and oblique comparisons. One blockhead talked of his deficiency in the female character — the very thing in which he and Shakespeare most excel.

Juliet herself may, for one moment, turn her eyes from Romeo on little Nell, and Desdemona take to heart her hairbreadth escapes. I dare not decide which of these three characters is the most interesting and pathetic.

BATH, *December* 21

PERMIT me to be quite vernacular, and to say, instead of *the compliments of the season*, "a merry Christmas!" How well that sounds — there are the village bells in it.

BATH, *October* 18, 1843

I DETEST the character of Rousseau, but I cannot resist his eloquence. He had more of it, and finer than any man. Demosthenes' was a contracted heart; and even Milton's was vitiated by the sourness of theology.

BATH, *November* 5, 1844

THE rheumatism you know (or rather I hope you do *not* know) always comes with a heavy cudgel. It was caused by my imprudence in rising up in my bed to fix a thought on paper — night is not the time to pin a butterfly on a blank leaf. Four hot baths have now almost buoyed up this monster from oppressing me. Of its four legs, I feel only one upon me, and indeed just the extremity of the hoof. At Gore House I should forget it — there I forgot the plague when I had it. But Bath air is the best in the world. In twenty minutes we can have three climates.

January 1, 1845

MOST things are real with me, except realities.

August 28, 1846

I FEEL I am growing old, for want of somebody to tell me (charming falsehood) that I am looking as young as ever. There is a vast deal of vital air in loving words.

January 9, 1849

I FEEL a great interest, a great anxiety, for the welfare of Louis Napoleon. I told him, if ever he were again in prison, I would visit him there; but never, if he were upon a throne, would I come near him. He is the only man living who would adorn one, but thrones are my aversion and abhorrence. France, I fear, can exist in no other condition. Her public men are greatly more able than ours, but they have less integrity. Every Frenchman is by nature an intriguer. It was not always so, to the same extent; but nature is modified, and even changed, by circumstances. Even garden statues take their form from clay.

(To John Forster)

December 21, 1840

IN this weather nobody can be quite well. I myself, an oddly-mixt metal with a pretty large portion of iron in it, am sensible to the curse of climate. The chief reason is, I cannot walk through the snow and slop. My body, and my mind more especially, requires strong exercise. Nothing can tire either, excepting dull people, and they weary both at once. The snow fell in Italy at the end of November, and the weather was severe at Florence. Lately, from the want of sun and all things cheerful, my saddened and wearied mind has often roosted on the acacias and cypresses I planted. Thoughts when they're weakest take the longest flights, and tempt the wintry seas in darkest nights. How is it that when I am a little melancholy my words are apt to fall into verse? Joy has never such an effect on me. In fact, we hardly speak when we meet, and are at best but bowing acquaintance.

1844

A HERD of clownish Warwickshire squires of the purest breed, and in no county of England is the breed so pure, was resolved to celebrate Shakespeare's birthday at Stratford-upon-Avon. I was invited: I declined. I told them he was not only the greatest glory of their county but the greatest work of God's creation, but I should hardly testify my love and veneration by eating and drinking, and I had refused all such invitations when I might meet those who knew me, of whom in Warwickshire there is now scarcely one. I could not help doubting whether any of the party ever read a single page of his writings; but I entertain no doubt whatever that if he were living and had come into the party, they would have butted him out. As the rocks that bound the sea are formed by the smallest and most inert insects, so celebrity seems to rise up from accretions equally vile and worthless. This idea has occurred to me many times before, and may perhaps be found in my writings; but never did it come forward with so luminous a stare as on the present occasion.

1856

I HAVE been cushioning my old head on the pillow of novels. What a delightful book is Bulwer's *Caxtons!* I have done him injustice, for I never thought he could have written such pure Saxon English as may be found here; and Sterne himself, whom he has chosen to imitate as to manner, is hardly better in the way of character. *Esmond*, too, is a novel that has surprised me. Never could I have believed that Thackeray, great as his abilities are, could have written so noble a story as *Esmond*. On your recommendation I have since been reading the whole of *Humphrey Clinker*. It seems to me that I must have read a part of it before. Every letter ends with *rigmarole*, then much in fashion, and thought to be very graceful. By rigmarole I mean such a termination as this: "It had like to have kindled the flames of discord in the family of yours always, etc." A tail always curls round the back of the letter-writer, and sticks to his *sincerely*, etc. How would Cicero and Pliny and Trajan have laughed at this circumbendibus! In the main, however, you are right about the book. It has abundant humour; and how admirable are such strokes as where the jailer's wife "wishes there was such another good soul in every jail in England!" . . . I must now run to Dickens for refreshment. He is a never-failing resource; and what an astonishing genius he is!

1856

I HAVE been out of doors not more than twice in fifty-nine days, a few minutes in each. I think I will go and die in Italy, but not in my old home. It is pleasant to see the sun about one's death-bed. . . .

Three months hence I shall once more purchase a landed property, situated in the parish of Widcombe, and comprising by actual admeasurement eight feet by four, next adjoining the church-tower in said parish. No magpie drapery, no lead, no rascals in hatbands, no horses in full feathers for me. Six old chairmen are sufficient. I thought once of complying with your kind wish that I should lie at Tachbrook, but I am not worth the carriage so far. And now again, about dying. Out of my hundred pounds, when I get it, I will reserve ten for my funeral, with strict orders that the sum may not be exceeded; and the gravestone and grave will amount to nearly or quite ten more. As I can live without superfluities, surely I can die without them.

1856

I TAKE it uncivil in Death to invite and then to balk me. It was troublesome to walk back, when I found he would not take me in. I do hope and trust he will never play me the same trick again. We ought both of us to be graver.

The Old Lion

Charles Dickens to his old friend

(To Walter Savage Landor)

PARIS, *November* 22, 1846

YOUNG MAN, — I will not go there if I can help it. I have not the least confidence in the value of your introduction to the Devil. I can't help thinking that it would be of better use "the other way, the other way," but I won't try it there, either, at present, if I can help it. Your godson says, is that your duty? and he begs me to enclose a blush newly blushed for you.

As to writing, I have written to you twenty times and twenty more to that, if you only knew it. I have been writing a little Christmas book, besides, expressly for you. And if you don't like it, I shall go to the font of Marylebone Church as soon as I conveniently can and renounce you: I am not to be trifled with. I write from Paris. I am getting up some French steam. I intend to proceed upon the longing-for-a-lap-of-blood-at-last principle, and if you *do* offend me, look to it.

We are all well and happy, and they send loves to you by the bushel. We are in the agonies of house-hunting. The people are frightfully civil, and grotesquely extortionate. One man (with a house to let) told me yesterday that he loved the Duke of Wellington like a brother. The same gentleman wanted to hug me round the neck with one hand, and pick my pocket with the other.

Don't be hard upon the Swiss. They are a thorn in the sides of European despots, and a good wholesome people to live near Jesuit-ridden kings on the brighter side of the mountains. My hat shall ever be ready to be thrown up, and my glove ever be ready to be thrown down, for Switzerland. If you were the man I took you for, when I took you (as a godfather) for better and for worse, you would come to Paris and amaze the weak walls of the house I haven't found yet with that steady snore of yours, which I once heard piercing the door of your bedroom in Devonshire Terrace, reverberating along the bell wire in the hall, so getting outside into the street, playing Æolian harps among the area railings, and going down the New Road like the blast of a trumpet.

I forgive you your reviling of me: there's a shovelful of live coals for your head — does it burn? And am, with true affection — does it burn now? — Ever yours.

CHARLES DICKENS

XVI

LACONICS

The Sailor and the King

(Jack Skifton to Charles II

KING CHARLES, — One of your subjects, the other night, robbed me of forty pounds, for which I robbed another of the same sum, who has inhumanly sent me to Newgate, and he swears I shall be hanged; therefore, for your own sake, save my life, or you will lose one of the best seamen in your navy.

JACK SKIFTON

(The Reply)

JACK SKIFTON, — For this time I'll save thee from the gallows; but if hereafter thou art guilty of the like, by —— I'll have thee hanged, though the best seaman in my navy. — Thine, CHARLES REX

Anne, Countess of Dorset, speaks her mind to Sir Joseph Williamson, Secretary of State under Charles II

SIR, — I have been bullied by an usurper, I have been illtreated by a court, but I won't be dictated to by a subject. Your man shall not stand.

ANN DORSET, PEMBROKE AND MONTGOMERY

Garrick and his factotum

(W. Stone to David Garrick)

I

Thursday noon

SIR, — Mr. Lacy turned me out of the lobby yesterday, and behaved very ill to me — I only ax'd for my two guineas for the last Bishop, and he swore I should not have a farthing. I cannot live upon air. I have a few Cupids you may have cheap, as they belong to a poor journeyman shoemaker, who I drink with now and then. — I am your humble Servant, W. STONE

II

Friday morning

STONE, — You are the best fellow in the world — bring the Cupids to the Theatre to-morrow; if they are under six, and well made, you shall have a guinea a-piece for them. Mr. Lacy will pay you himself for the Bishop — he is very penitent for what he has done: if you can get me two murderers, I will pay you handsomely, particularly the spouting fellow who keeps the apple-stand on Tower-hill; the cut in his face is just the thing. Pick me up an alderman or two for Richard, if you can; and I have no objection to treat with you for a comely Mayor. The Barber will not do for Brutus, although I think he will succeed in Mat. D. G.

III

SIR, — The Bishop of Winchester is getting drunk at the *Bear* — and swears he will not play to-night. — I am yours, W. STONE

IV

STONE, — The Bishop may go to the devil; I do not know a greater rascal, except yourself. D. G.

Captain Walton wastes no words

(To Admiral Byng)

SIR, — We have taken and destroyed all the Spanish ships and vessels which were upon the coast, the number as per margin. — I am, etc., G. WALTON

Taken. — Admiral Mari, and four men of war, of 60, 54, 40, and 24 guns; a ship laden with arms, and a bomb vessel. Burnt. — Four men of war, of 54, 40, and 30 guns; a fire ship, and a bomb vessel.

"*Canterbury*," off Syracusa, *August* 16, 1718

William Cowper acknowledges a gift of cloth

(To Lady Hesketh)

I THANK you for the snip of cloth, commonly called a pattern. At present I have two coats and but one back. If at any time hereafter I should find myself possessed of fewer coats and more backs, it will be of use to me.

The loans that failed

I

Mrs. Foote to her son the actor

DEAR SON, — I am in prison for debt; come and assist your loving mother. E. FOOTE

The Reply

DEAR MOTHER, — So am I; which prevents his duty being paid to his loving mother. — Your affectionate son, SAMUEL FOOTE

P.S. — I have sent my attorney to assist you; in the meantime let us hope for better days.

II

Beau Brummel to Scrope Davies

MY DEAR SCROPE, — Lend me two hundred pounds. The banks are shut and all my money is in the three per cents. It shall be repaid to-morrow morning. — Yours, GEORGE BRUMMEL

The Reply

MY DEAR GEORGE, — 'Tis very unfortunate, but all my money is in the three per cents. — Yours,

S. DAVIES

III

One provincial actor to another

DEAR W., — Lend me a couple of shillings until Saturday, and oblige. — Yours, ——

P.S. — On second thoughts, make it three.

The Reply

DEAR JACK, — I have only one shilling myself, or would oblige. — Yours, ——

P.S. — On second thoughts, I must change that for dinner.

Charles Napier ("Black Charles") asks for a ship

(To the First Lord of the Admiralty)

1810

SIR, — My leave of absence is just out. I don't think it worth remaining here, for I expect you will give me a ship, as I am almost tired of campaigning, which is a damned rum concern.

C. N.

The candidate and the voter

Mr. J. G. Lambton, contesting Durham, to Sir Thomas Liddell

February 28, 1820

MY DEAR SIR, — In times like the present, it is impossible to allow private feelings to take place of a public sense of duty. I think your conduct as dangerous in Parliament as it is in your own county. Were you my own brother, therefore, I could not give you my support.

THOMAS LIDDELL

The Reply

MY DEAR SIR THOMAS, — In answer to your letter, I beg to say that I feel gratitude for your frankness, compassion for your fears, little dread of your opposition, and no want of your support. — I am, etc.,

J. G. LAMBTON

The Rev. Sydney Smith accepts an invitation conditionally

May 14, 1842

MY DEAR DICKENS, — I accept your obliging invitation conditionally. If I am invited by any man of greater genius than yourself, or one by whose works I have been more completely interested, I will repudiate you, and dine with the more splendid phenomenon of the two. — Ever yours sincerely,

SYDNEY SMITH

Walter Savage Landor to Lord Normanby, who had cut him

[*circa* 1858]

MY LORD, — Now I am recovering from an illness of several months' duration, aggravated no little by your lordship's rude reception of me at the Cascine, in presence of my family and innumerable Florentines, I must remind you in the gentlest terms of the occurrence.

We are both of us old men, my lord, and are verging on decrepitude and imbecility. Else my note might be more energetic. I am not unobservant of distinctions. You by the favour of a minister are Marquis of Normanby, I by the grace of God am

WALTER SAVAGE LANDOR

Louis Duchosal, the Genevese poet, writes to Paul Verlaine introducing a disciple

AMI, — Je t'envoie Pierre Paul Plan, poète. Dis lui des choses,

DUCHOSAL

An old lady sends her nephew a present

MY DEAR NEPHEW, — I am sending you some of your favourite cherries, preserved in brandy so that they may keep. I hope you and your friends will enjoy them. — Your affectionate aunt.

The Reply

MY DEAR AUNT, — A thousand thanks for your kind gift. I appreciate the cherries immensely, not so much for themselves, as for the spirit in which they are sent. — Your affectionate nephew.

Master George Wells, after an operation, informs Master Frank Wells of his duty

DEAR FRANK, — I hope you will not think me selfish, but I am in such great pain that I think you ought to get me a small present. — Your loving

GEORGE

A commercial traveller, after a boisterous absence from work, inquires as to his status

DEAR FIRM, am I still with you?

XVII

WHIMSICALITIES

A farmer's daughter is forced to decline ~ ~

[1798]

DEAR MISS, — The energy of the races prompts me to assure you that my request is forbidden, the idea of which I had awkwardly nourished, notwithstanding my propensity to reserve. Mr. T. will be there. Let me with confidence assure you that him and brothers will be very happy to meet you and brothers. Us girls cannot go for reasons. The attention of the cows claims our assistance in the evening. — Unalterably yours,

——

A Quaker schoolboy (aged 13) is dutiful to his parents ~ ~ ~ ~ ~ ~

GODMANCHESTER, 14 : 11 Mo. 1743

HONOURED MOTHER, — Thy very kind Epistle of the 7th instant, with the Present of Pyes and Cakes, I duly and safely received and gratefully acknowledge, was much pleased to hear you were in a Measure of health, a good Degree whereof divine providence is favouring my Self and the generality of our Family with at this present writing, and heartily desire may be continued to you and us with dear Father in his Travels and Return home to you again. With the cordial Tenders of Duty to thy Self and dear Father, of kind Love to Sisters with all other Relations and enquiring Friends to all whom Master and family desire to be kindly remembered Shall conclude and as in Duty bound subscribe my Self. — Thy dutiful Son,

WILLIAM IMPEY

Miss Pelham's maid, Mrs. Maxwell, has to refuse an invitation

MRS. MAXWELL presents her respects to Mrs. Stanley. She is at once both happy and uneasy at her kind remembrance. She is very sorry she cannot wait on Mrs. Stanley at that hour, as Miss Pelham dresses for both Courts that morning, returns home and dresses again for the Opera in the Evening, so that she shall be obliged to forego the mortification of that satisfaction. She wishes Mrs. Stanley every pleasure the Opera can afford, and setting apart such transient joys every substantial bliss you merit.

Lord Stormont and Sir James Scarlett crave the social influence of the ladies of Norwich

[1832]

TO THE LADIES OF NORWICH, — "None but the brave deserve the fair." — If ever the sweets of social virtue, the wrath of honest zeal, the earnings of industry, and the prosperity of Trade, had any influence in the female breast, you have now a happy opportunity of exercising it to the advantage of *your* country — *your* cause.

If ever the feelings of a parent, wife, sister, friend, or lover, had a sympathy with *public virtue*, now is *your* time to indulge the *fonder passion.* If ever you felt for the ruin and disgrace of England, and for the *miseries and deprivations* occasioned by the obnoxious Reform Bill, you are called on, by the most tender and affectionate tie in nature, to exert *your* persuasive influence on the mind of a father, brother, husband, or lover: tell them not to seek filial duty, congenial regard, matrimonial comfort, nor *tender compliance*, till they have saved *your* country from *perdition* — *posterity* from *slavery!* History furnishes us with instances of *female patriotism* equal to any in the page of *war* and politics. O! may the generous and beatific charms of female persuasion prevail with the *citizens of Norwich*, to espouse the cause of real liberty — of STORMONT AND SCARLETT

The Six Misses Montgomerie (daughters of the Earl of Eglinton) ask a boon of Lord Milton

THE Petition of the Six Vestal Virgins of Eglinton to the Honourable Lord Milton.

Humbly sheweth — that whereas your petitioners has taken upon them to solicite in behalf of Alexander Aickenhead, part of whose storie your Lordship knows already. His new misfortune is, that after he had received sentence of banishment for three years out of this regality, he was unhappily seduced by his principal creditors to come privetly to his own house to compound some debts, but was not an hour there before the malitious neighbourhood inform'd against him, and had him unexpectedly apprehended and carried to Irvine gaol; So we being importun'd by his wife (who is extremely handsome), join'd with our own inclinations to serve the poor man, we're in hopes that these two motives will have some ascendant over your lordship's natural disposition to relieve the distress'd; and to excite you still further to this good action, his wife, as the only acceptible reward she thinks she can make for this piece of humanity she hopes from your lordship in favour of her husband's liberty, she protests you shall have as many kisses as you please to demand (and we likewise bind and oblige ourselves to do the same, when your lordship makes your publick entrie here in May); but we once more beg you'll use your interest to get the man out of prison, which you'll do a particular good to his family and an infinite obligation to your pupils, whose ambition's to subscribe themselves. — Your lordship's most affectionate children,

Bettie Montgomerie
Eleanor Montgomerie
Susanna Montgomerie
Mary Montgomerie
Frances Montgomerie
Christian Montgomerie

P.S. — We'll esteem it a favour if your lordship will honour us with an answer. But for heaven's sake remember that the wife is hansom.

A gentle lady puts a firm to the pain of selling her something

GENTLEMEN, — Will you, of your kindness, pardon the liberty I take in venturing to trouble you with a small request, being a stranger to you. But my sister, Mrs. Avenell, lately residing at Bellevue, Medina Road, Brightburne, intimated to me that you would very likely be so good as not to object to my requesting a small favour from you, and I have ventured to ask in that belief. If, therefore, I am not presuming too much, might I ask the kind favour of a black velvet-spotted veil being sent to me? The pattern I venture to enclose is from a veil my sister sent me from your establishment, and it is so superior to those I obtain here, in softness and thickness of the spots, that I should much like another, as near to it as convenient. I think the one yard and a little more came to about one and sixpence. It is the soft quality which I like, combined with the close thick spots.

I will, if you are so good as to entertain my request, send postal order previously to the receipt of the parcel.

Awaiting your kind reply, with many apologies if I have troubled you inconveniently, Believe me to be, Gentlemen, Yours respectfully, ——

A true Protestant objects to "Wolsey" underwear

January 8, 1908

DEAR SIRS, — I am sorry to return the Drawers, which are a trifle too small round the waist.

At the expense of being considered bigoted, to tell you the truth, I do not like the Brand, although the material is excellent in quality.

The man whose likeness appears, "WOLSEY," was one under whom poor Protestants *writhed*, and although you may say this is a small matter and of no importance, it indicates the Firm at least allowing such to go forth in these critical times is at least careless, if not genuine Roman Catholics, and a Feather will indicate which way the wind blows.

Again the buttons would be far better of linen instead of pearl. Please to send me others. — Believe me, Yours faithfully,

——

A belligerent changes his mind

DEAR SIR, — I write to tell you that I shall not take the remaining ten of my dozen boxing lessons with you. My reason for taking your course was, as I told you, because I have been promised a thrashing by Mr. —— when he catches me. I have come to the conclusion that I would rather have his than yours. I cannot thank you for the pains you have taken, because I did all the taking, didn't I? — Yours,

——

A Chinese editor is under the painful necessity of refusing a contribution

ILLUSTRIOUS brother of the sun and moon — Behold thy servant prostrate before thy feet. I kowtow to thee and beg that of thy graciousness thou mayest grant that I may speak and live. Thy honoured manuscript has deigned to cast the light of its august countenance upon me. With raptures I have perused it. By the bones of my ancestors, never have I encountered such wit, such pathos, such lofty thought. With fear and trembling I return the writing. Were I to publish the treasure you sent me, the Emperor would order that it should be made the standard, and that none be published except such as equalled it. Knowing literature as I do, and that it would be impossible in ten thousand years to equal what you have done, I send your writing back. Ten thousand times I crave your pardon. Behold my head is at your feet. Do what you will. — Your servant's servant,

THE EDITOR

A great Victorian is beset by a poor artist

August 9

MR. FRITH having given me ten shillings altogether, if he would give me half-sovereign it would make me proud. I would withdraw any request which might not meet Mr. Frith's intentions; there fore, at the outside, would ask Mr. Frith to give me ten shillings, and I would not repeat any requests for twelve months, not asking Mr. Frith for money at a larger scale than one pound a year. A half-sovereign would purchase a good deal of bread for a short time. Insufficient supply of bread, and no butter is what I complain of. Two great hungry boys and three girls. I am only desirous of getting the drawing and painting in motion, as may be seen from a note-book which I have in my pocket, which contains a pen-and-ink sketch of Her Majesty the Queen, that, carved with effect, would be a group of the royal family.

A long time back I inquired as to how I might get an interview with the Prince of Wales. I was told to write to Fisher the Secretary, but he was not in town. This was three years back. I thought his royal highness might give me a regular income if he thought I was capable of holding the post of painter in ordinary. Such an office David Wilkie held. David Wilkie was a bachelor, and had no interruptions to his pursuits. I thought it not safe to have anything sent to me to the B—— post office, because I suspected that it might be stolen — I am very suspicious. I think there is temptation to purloin when they think the party addressed is an easy person not likely to kick up a row. Some of these postmasters have known vicissitudes, and unless a man has the highest principles, could not resist the temptation. I had not pluck to call upon the people to ask them for money — not as yet. I pass and repass their houses without having pluck to call and ask for anything, caused partly by a rebuff I received from Mr. C. of B——, for he said, "Cut it short" (my message); and added in my hearing, not to me, but to the servant, "Tell him I have enough to do with my own people."

If Mr. Frith sent me the money, would he please to put it in a cut card by registered letter? The reason I make the application is this: I dreamt that Mr. Frith, or some one, sent me that amount; perhaps he would make the said dream come true.

Mr. Frith might take it into his head to send me one pound once in twelve months, either in four or two parts, or at once, I promising not to tease Mr. Frith until September 1870. Perhaps by that time my position might be considerably altered as regards pecuniary difficulties.

Perhaps this is the last note for twelve months at least I shall trouble you with. What's the good of wasting paper and one's time for nothing? — I am yours respectfully, ——

Mr. Henwood asks a variety of assistance of the Rev. A. Blomfield

10 BUTTER STREET, BETHNAL GREEN
February 2, 1866

REV. AND DEAR SIR, — I regret to inform you that I am ill from grief, having grieved at your Departure, sustaining thereby a heavy loss, as you were a *kind*, and one of my *best* customers for wine, etc., you having taken of me *ever* since the early part '64, you having kindly given me a Testimonial respecting the Pale Sherry and Brandy dated April 1864. I shall be deeply grateful, nay I humbly *Pray* that you may be graciously pleased to listen to my cry, and grant my *Petition*, namely that you should kindly give me an order that I may live and not die, and a mine of gratitude, Dear Sir, shall be sprung, which *Death alone* can exhaust.

I pray that my necessity may be a sufficient apology for this Intrusion, and that my extremity may be God's opportunity, through your Instrumentality, and to Father, Son, and Holy Ghost all praise and glory shall redound. — I beg to remain, Yours faithfully till death, most humbly imploring a line, C. W. HENWOOD

P.S. — I shall be happy to come and clean your windows for you outside for *nothing*, should you please, having done them for the Rev. J. Strickland M.A. of St. Jude's Whitechapel. I have also had the honour to serve with Brandy the Rev. Francis Blomfield M.A.

P.S. — Dear Sir, I am at present in a most wretched and Deplorable state of mind; the Tempter as tempted me, life seems a blank to me. Oh if you could but know how unhappy I am, I am sure you would pity and help me. I have struggled against adversity; I ask an interest in your Prayers. Probably you may be able to give me an order for a gallon of Brandy.

(*Written on the envelope*)

DEAR SIR, whenever the word Beaujolais is mentioned I shall always think of you.

An old Irish farmer desires the custom of an honourable solvent butter-merchant

I

PERMIT me to say that the butter produced from off of the fertile Lands and the Daisy Clad hillocks of this Romantic Parish and having it manufactured by the Lilly white hands of an Amiable Excellent Lady that it must be of Incomparable Excellence sufficient to give delectation to the Taste and Olfactory Nerve of the Honorable and Exquisite Epicures. Permit me to solicit your honor to Exhibit this test firkin of Butter in your Superb Establishment as a paragon of Taste and Pulcritude, proving itself to be far sweeter and more mellifluent than the Remarkable dews that fell in the days of Yore on the mountains of Sion.

II

HON[BLE] SIR, — The many acts of dignified Generosity which have characterized your honor thro' life, the tender, Just, and Feeling disposition your Honor has Evinced thro' Life in all Communications addressed to your Honor, and the Natural Tendency to promote and Effect the Goodness and Kindness which predominates Triumphantly in your honor's Noble, pure, and Exalted bosom, prompted me, a Venerable Ballyhildrum Farmer to address your Honor, hoping that my appeal will not be Frustrated but will meet with your Honor's approval and Kind Consideration.

III

HONBLE SIR, — I Received your Honor's Kind, and Complimentary letter which has Excited my spirits, to an unlimited state of Ecstasy which I return your Honor my Sincere and unfeigned thanks for Giving your Honor's orders to the Clanmally Butter Factory at my request, for one firkin of Butter as a Test firkin, why your Honor it would delight the heart, and charm the eye of any person to see the daisy clad Hillocks and shamrock fields of this Romantic Parish. . . .

I am 81 years of age last August and out of pure Love, and Friendship for your Honor, please permit me to solicit your Honor — For my last Request, to Enclose your Honor's photograph, and the Photograph of your Honor's Amiable Lovely, and Excellent Lady, to me, I'll Treasure and Keep them hung up in my parlour as paragons of Beauty, and Loveliness.

And in Return I'll Wield my pen tho' old I am, bestowing deserving Eulogy on your Honor, And on your Honor's Amiable, Lovely and Excellent Lady.

IV

HON^{BLE} SIR, — I received your Honors and Honble Lady's Photographs this morning, which I Return your Honor and Honble Lady, my Sincere and Unfeigned thanks for the favour and Honor bestowed on me, a favor and Honor, I'll appreciate thro' Life.

It's not the Photograph I admire tho' it being Beautiful Chaste, Exquisite, and Intrinsically Grand present of art and taste, and it Borrows all its Lustre and Value from the Honble Feelings that called it forth, and the humane affectionate Regard and Respect, that accompanied the present, feelings I'll thro' Life cherish, and it puts a Greater Crown on the present and enchances it one hundred times more and more as an Humble Co. Cork Farmer to be Dignified with such an Honble Exquisite Present.

First of all when I look at your Honor's Photograph it explicitly indicates to me, that your Honor is the Type of a Nobleman, having Alacrity depicted on your Honor's Countenance and Benevolence in your heart, and your honor is thro' Life Benefiscent and Charitable Condescending and humane, your honor is thro' Life a Noble, Illustrious, Magnanimous, and Philanthropic Nobleman, who is Loved and Beloved by all, Respected by the great and Noble of the Land, Your Honor being a Goodhearted, Kindhearted, Noblehearted unobtrusive Nobleman who have supported An Immaculate character Thro' Life.

Your Honor is a Nobleman, who is broad and clear of Views, decisive and Energetic of Action seeing at a

Glance your Means and Ends, and Ignoring the Idea of failure, your Honor is courteous of demeanour, Charitable in word and work, Honble and Equitable in all your dealings thro' life, as a beloved Husband, A Kind, fond, and Affectionate parent, a first class Butter, and Bacon Merchant, and a warmhearted Friend, why your Honor is a Model Man — your Honor is the Life and Soul of progress, you are a nobleman of Immense Business powers, and the Brilliancy of your Honor's mind and character, could only be compared to the (Sun) on his Evening declination when he Remits his Splendour, but Retains his Magnitude, and pleases more tho' he dazzles less, and the saying of the poet is Verified in your Honor that you are of the first flowers of the Earth, and first Gem of the Sea.

But your Honor do not Require my simple Eulogy to Enhance your Honor's merits or my Lowly and Unadorned Language to portray your Honor's Inestimable Qualifications.

Secondly, I have to Bestow a share of deserved Eulogy on the Honble Lovely Lady Dixon, as follows —

First of all, The Scripture says, that a good Wife is a good Fortune, And that houses, Lands, and Cash are Given by parents, but that a prudent, Lovely, Amiable, and Excellent Lady, is properly from the Lord. Such as the Lovely, Amiable Lady Dixon is, why to Look at her Ladyship's face, You'll see that Heaven has implanted something beyond this world, Something bearing Kindred with the Skys on her Ladyship, The Angelical appearance the Beautiful Golden Looking Hair, fine high Forehead, Smiling Countenance, Milk White Breast, and Stately deportment, that Providence and Nature, have blessed her Ladyship with And her Ruby

Lips and Fragrant breath is far sweeter and more mellifluent than the Remarkable Dews that fell in the days of Yore, on the Mountains of Sion. I Congratulate your Honor, to be Allied in the Rosy path of Matrimony to such an Amiable, Lovely, and Excellent Lady, because in her Ladyship's Juvenile days she was in Beauty and Bloom by a true Comparison to be chosen by a King or to be a prince's companion and vincet veritas. Her Ladyship is Young, tall, and straight, Neat and handsome, Supreme in Knowledge and Female Carriage, sweet odour flows from her head to her Ladyship's toes.

Her Ladyship is Nature's pride by the height of Morality, she being Endowed with Charity and Hospitality, Sweet odour flows from her Head to her Ladyship's toes. And Secondly her Ladyship is Nature's pride, and Nature, as if desirous that so bright a production of her Skill should shine forth, has bestowed on the Honble Lady Dixon Bodily Accomplishments, Vigour of Limbs, Dignity of shape and Air, and a pleasing Engaging and Open Cheerful Countenance.

Honble Sir, and Madam, please Excuse this long Extemporary Letter, Wishing may Providence diffuse his choicest Blessings on Your Honor and Honble Lady, And on Your Young Lovely Family, And may ye all be blessed with Length of days and Years in Good Health — Amen.

Hoping when Your Honor will Receive this Cherished Letter please don't allow it to go astray, But like the Polar Star above will shine in print in Your Honor's Lovely Parlour every day. — Believe me, Honble Sir And Madam, With Profound Respect, Your Obt Servant, Most Respectfully, ——

XVIII

OLLA PODRIDA

Bishop Warburton preaches philosophy to the Rev. Dr. Stukely

June 19, 1738

MY DEAR FRIEND, — I beg your acceptance of the inclosed. Our friend the Doctor told me he had the pleasure of seeing you. He told me, you rejected the lines he shewed you as impostures. I do not wonder at it. You know best whether the thing be possible. But the family is so far above all suspicion of fraud, or having any ends to serve by it, that nothing but an absolute impossibility could make me disbelieve it.

I hope you are easier in your domestics than you was; that you have got servants that are honest, careful, and with a few brains. I very much wish to see you, and hope you will do me that pleasure at Broughton some time next month. However, do me the favour to let me know, that I may be at home; for this summer time I have some short excursion or other that I am every post making, but none half so interesting to me as the seeing you. I hope the young ones are all well, and that Miss Fanny is grown woman enough now to make your coffee; a happiness, some years ago, you used to flatter yourself with the hopes of living to see.

You see the burthen of my song is hope, hope, hope;

and how much I am obliged to live upon it. But, that this may never fool you or me too long, I will tell you a story. Sir Francis Bacon was walking out one evening near the Thames, where he saw some fishermen ready to cast in their nets: he asked them what they would have for their draught; they said, ten shillings; he bade them five; so, not agreeing, the fishermen threw in upon their own fortune, and took nothing. On this, Bacon seeing them look very blank, asked them why they were such blockheads as not to take his money? They answered, they had been toiling all day, and had taken nothing, and they were in *hopes* that their last cast would have made amends for all: on which he told them, they were unlucky dogs; but that he would give them something to carry home with them; and it was this maxim, which they should be sure never to forget, *That hope is a good breakfast, but a very bad supper.* So far for my story. But I do not know how it is; but I should make but a bad meal of it, either at breakfast or supper. I should like it well enough for a kind of second course, as cheese to digest a good substantial dinner. And so the happy use it; while the unhappy, like the poor, are forced to make an eternal meal upon it. — I am, dear friend, yours most affectionately,
W. WARBURTON

Dr. Andrew Brown (?) instils worldly wisdom into Scotch physicians

DEAR SIR, — I thank you for the present of your small Treatise about Vomiting in Fevers, but at the same time I approve of your reasons, you must give me leave to condemn your conduct: I know you begin to storm at this; but have a little patience. There was a physician of this town, perhaps the most famous in his time, being called to his patient, complaining (it may be) of an oppression at his stomach; he would very safely and cautiously order him a decoction of *carduus*, sometimes hot water; I don't know but he would allow now and then fat mutton broth too. The patient was vomited, and the doctor could justifie himself that he had not omitted that necessary evacuation; this was his constant practice. Being chid by his collegues, who well knew he neglected antimony, not out of ignorance or fear, he would roguishly tell them, "Come, come, gentlemen, that might cure my patient, but it would kill the distemper, and I should have less money in my pocket. A pretty business indeed, a rich citizen overgorges himself, which by management may be improved into a good substantial fever, worth at least twenty guineas; and you would have me nip the plant in the bud, have a guinea for my pains, and lose the reputation of a safe practitioner to boot." The gentleman had reason, all trades must live. Alas! our people here are grown too quick-sighted, they will have antimonial vomits, and a physician dares not omit them, tho' it is many a good fee out of his pocket. Join, I say, with these wise gentlemen; they wish well to the Faculty; procure an order of the Colledge, and banish antimony the city of Edinburgh, and the liberties thereof. 'Tis a barbarous thing in these hard times to strangle an infant distemper; they ought no more to be murdered than young cattle in Lent. Let it be as great a crime to kill a fever with an antimonial vomit, as to fish in spawning time. The Dutch physicians are like the rest of their nation wise; they banish that heathenish Jesuitical drug, that would quickly reduce their practice to a narrow compass in the hopefulest distemper of the countrey. These rogues that dream of nothing but specificks and panaceas, I would have them all hang'd, not so much for the folly of the attempt, as the malice of their intention; rascals, to starve so many worthy gentlemen, that perhaps know no otherwise to get their livelihood. Will the glasiers ever puzle themselves to make glass malleable, would the knitters ever so much as have dreamed of a stocking-loom, or the young writers petition'd to have informations printed; all those are wise in their generation, and must the physicians be the only fools?

We all know here there is no danger in antimonial vomits, but this is *inter nos;* you must not tell your patient so, let him believe, as I said before, that antimonial vomits are dangerous, deleterial, break the fibres of the stomach, etc., and that you cannot safely give them. So shall you be stiled a cautious, safe physician, one that won't spoil the curll of a man's hair to pull him out of the river. We have some dangerous dogs here, that in a quinsy, when a man is ready to be chock'd, will blood him forty ounces at once; is not this extreamly hazardous? They cut off limbs, cut for the stone; is this safe? I tell you the reputation of a wary safe physician is worth all the parts of his character besides. Now I hope you will allow I have reason for what I said.

I have seen the *Melius Inquirendum*, and am too well acquainted with the stile and spelling, not to know that it is Dr. Eyzat's; but here I must be with you again, how come you to write against one that says two drams of emetick wine is a sufficient doze for a man? Suffer not such things to come abroad; they will imagine you are not got so far as the circulation of the blood in Scotland; write seriously against such people. Fy upon't, I will never allow them to be above the dispensation of ballads and doggrel, etc. — I am, Sir, yours, etc.

LONDON, *August* 23, 1699

Lady Dufferin is whimsical on property

HAMPTON COURT, *October* 22

MY DEAR MISS BERRY, — I began a little note the other day to thank you for your kind remembrance of me and your coming so far to see me (which opportunity I was *very* sorry to have missed), but my note in the agitating agonies of packing up disappeared, and I had no strength of mind to begin another. My mother and I have returned to this place for a few days, in order to make an ineffectual grasp at any remaining property that we may have in the world. Of course you have heard that we were robbed and murdered the other night by a certain soft-spoken cook, who headed a storming party of banditti through my mother's kitchen window; if not, you will see the full, true, and dreadful particulars in the papers, as we are to be "had up" at the Old Bailey on Monday next for the trial. We have seen a great deal of life, and learnt a great deal of the criminal law of England this week, — knowledge cheaply purchased at the cost of all my wardrobe and all my mother's plate. We have gone through two examinations in court: they were very hurrying and agitating affairs, and I had to kiss either the Bible or the magistrate — I don't recollect which, but *it* smelt of thumbs. The magistrates seemed to take less interest in my clothes than in my mother's spoons; — I suppose from some secret *affinity* or *congeniality* which they were conscious of. "Similis gaudet" — something — (I have lost my Latin with the rest of my property). When I say "similis," I don't so much allude to the purity of the metal as to its particular form.

I find that the idea of personal property is a fascinating illusion, for our goods belong in fact to our country, and not to us; and that the petticoats and stockings which I have fondly imagined mine, are really the petticoats of Great Britain and Ireland. I am now and then indulged with a distant glimpse of my most necessary garments in the hands of different policemen; but "in this stage of the proceedings" may do no more than wistfully recognise them. Even on such occasions, the words of justice are, "Policeman B 25, produce *your* gowns;" "Letter A 36, identify *your* lace;" "Letter C, tie up *your* stockings." All this is harrowing to the feelings; but one cannot have everything in this life; we have obtained justice and can easily wait for a change of linen. Hopes are held out to us that at some vague period in the lapse of time we may be allowed a *wear* out of our raiment — at least, so much of it as may have resisted the wear and tear of justice; and my poor mother looks confidently forward to being restored to the bosom of her silver teapot. But I don't know; I begin to look upon all property with a philosophic eye as unstable in its nature and liable to all sorts of pawnbrokers. Moreover, the police and I have so long had my clothes in common, that I shall never feel at home in them again. To a virtuous mind the idea that Inspector Dowsett examined into all one's hooks and eyes, tapes and buttons, etc., is inexpressibly painful. But I cannot pursue that view of the subject. Let me hope, dear Miss Berry, that you feel for us as we really deserve, and that you wish me well "thro' my clothes," on Monday next. . . . Yours very truly,

HELEN A. DUFFERIN

Olla Podrida

Canon Ainger sends a Christmas hamper of good stories

(To Mrs. Horace Smith)

MASTER'S HOUSE, TEMPLE, E.C.
Christmas 1898

MY DEAR FRIEND, — "As the Festive Season again recurs, I have to solicit a renewal of that friendly confidence, which it will ever be my study to deserve. I hope to be able to supply you with some fine Chestnuts for the Christmas dinner, of which samples are inclosed. Joe Millers are cheap to-day." — I quote from my favourite grocer. Lily — that "plant and flower of light" (Ben Jonson) sends me a very gratifying account of you all, especially of Edward, who I understand is shortly to take Holy Orders. If he would wish me to sign his "Si quis," I shall be happy to do so — and hope he will not think I am "Si-quizzing" him. . . .

I heard a story lately of a Butler.

Party in a Country House. Maid dressing a guest's hair. *Guest:* "I hope, Parker, you are comfortable in your place." "Oh yes, Ma'am — the society downstairs is so superior. The Butler leads the conversation. He is such a refined man — indeed, quite scientific. He has been telling us all about Evolution, and we quite understand it now. He says we are all descended from Darwin."

By the way, did you hear of Mrs. Creighton (wife of the Bishop of London) addressing a great Mothers' Meeting at the East End of London on how to make home attractive and comfortable and so on. *Old Lady* at the conclusion to another old Lady, "Ah! it's all very well — but I should like to know what Mrs. Creighton does when old Mr. Creighton *comes home drunk*."

And this by a natural association of ideas reminds me of an epigram just sent me from Bristol. At Clevedon (where William and I once sat and smoked under the Church wall) there is a very High Church clergyman named Vicars Foote, who has been lately reprimanded by his Bishop for excessive Ritual. A flippant person puts into the offending parson's mouth the following retort,

> "I will not leave my benefice,
> Nor change the ways I've got.
> A Bishop's foot may be put down,
> A *Vicar's Foot* may not!"

I wonder if another Theological story has reached Sheffield yet — about the old Scotch lady who heard that in the Revised Version of the Lord's Prayer, the Revisers had substituted "Deliver us from the evil one" for "Deliver us from evil" — (as they *have* done, you know). The old lady replied, "Eh, Sirs — but he'll be sair uplifted!"

I have been in Scotland this year, and in Ireland, but I think most of the good stories have been told. By the way, if you want some good *old* stories, get ——'s recently published volume of Rummy-nuisances (this is my witty way of spelling it). I have suggested (not to *him*) as a motto for the next Edition —

> Under the Chestnut Tree
> Who loves to lie with me?

As we are on the subject of the clergy, have you ever heard *this?* Scotch Minister returning to his Manse in the gloaming, becomes aware of a figure sleeping sweetly in a ditch. On further examination, he discovers one of his own Elders. After dragging him up and restoring his suspended animation, he asks, with some indignation, where his Church Officer had been. "Well, Minister, I canna weel remember whether it was a wedding or a Funeral — *but it was a gran' success!*" It must have been the same gentleman (or one of the same pattern), who at a dinner party, after drinking champagne during the earlier courses, was heard to murmur: "I hope there's some whisky coming! I get vera tired of these *mineral waters!*"

And now that you, like this gentleman, are getting "vera tired" of so much prose — and that, *not* sparkling — what say you to dropping into poetry like Mr. Wegg?

"There was an old man of Bengal
Who purchased a Bat and a Ball
Some gloves, and some pads —
(It was one of his fads —
For he never played cricket at all!)."

. . . Well, I fear you and yours will have to mourn over me that years do not seem to "bring the philosophic mind," and that your poor friend is just as frivolous as he was thirty years ago. Well, well, it's Christmas time, and a few Crackers (besides *Tom Smith's*) may be allowed upon the dinner table, among the plainer and more wholesome viands. And so I trust to be forgiven, and to be thought kindly of by my dear old friends at the "Westwood Arms," for that is *still* its name to me, knowing that they are always open to receive their attached and faithful friend. A. A.

R. L. S. has an Edinburgh adventure

(To Mrs. Sitwell, now Mrs. Sidney Colvin)

April 1875

HERE is my long story: yesterday night, after having supped, I grew so restless that I was obliged to go out in search of some excitement. There was a half-moon lying over on its back, and incredibly bright in the midst of a faint grey sky set with faint stars: a very inartistic moon, that would have damned a picture.

At the most populous place of the city I found a little boy, three years old perhaps, half frantic with terror, and crying to every one for his "Mammy." This was about eleven, mark you. People stopped and spoke to him, and then went on, leaving him more frightened than before. But I and a good-humoured mechanic came up together; and I instantly developed a latent faculty for setting the hearts of children at rest. Master Tommy Murphy (such was his name) soon stopped crying, and allowed me to take him up and carry him; and the mechanic and I trudged away along Princes Street to find his parents. I was soon so tired that I had to ask the mechanic to carry the bairn; and you should have seen the puzzled contempt with which he looked at me, for knocking in so soon. He was a good fellow, however, although very impracticable and sentimental; and he soon bethought him that Master Murphy might catch cold after his excitement, so we wrapped him up in my greatcoat. "Tobauga (Tobago) Street" was the address he gave us; and we deposited him in a little grocer's shop and went through all the houses in the street without being able to find any one of the name of Murphy. Then I set off to the head police office, leaving my greatcoat in pawn about Master Murphy's person. As I went down one of the lowest streets in the town, I saw a little bit of life that struck me. It was now half-past twelve, a little shop stood still half-open, and a boy of four or five years old was walking up and down before it imitating cockcrow. He was the only living creature within sight.

At the police offices no word of Master Murphy's parents; so I went back empty-handed. The good groceress, who had kept her shop open all this time, could keep the child no longer; her father, bad with bronchitis, said he must forth. So I got a large scone with currants in it, wrapped my coat about Tommy, got him up on my arm, and away to the police office with him: not very easy in my mind, for the poor child, young as he was — he could scarce speak — was full of terror for the "office," as he called it. He was now very grave and quiet and communicative with me; told me how his father thrashed him, and divers household matters. Whenever he saw a woman on our way he looked after her over my shoulder and then gave his judgment: "That's no *her*," adding sometimes, "She has a wean wi' her." Meantime I was telling him how I was going to take him to a gentleman who would find out his mother for him quicker than ever I could, and how he must not be afraid of him, but be brave, as he had been with me. We had just arrived at our destination — we were just under the lamp — when he looked me in the face and said appealingly, "He'll no put me in the office?" And I had to assure him that he would not, even as I pushed open the door and took him in.

The serjeant was very nice, and I got Tommy comfortably seated on a bench, and spirited him up with good words and the scone with the currants in it; and then, telling him I was just going out to look for Mammy, I got my greatcoat and slipped away.

Poor little boy! he was not called for, I learn, until ten this morning. This is very ill-written, and I've missed half that was picturesque in it; but to say truth, I am very tired and sleepy: it was two before I got to bed. However, you see, I had my excitement.

Monday. — I have written nothing all morning; I cannot settle to it. Yes — I *will* though.

10.45. — And I did. I want to say something more to you about the three women. I wonder so much why they should have been *women*, and halt between two opinions in the matter. Sometimes I think it is because they were made by a man for men; sometimes, again, I think there is an abstract reason for it, and there is something more substantive about a woman than ever there can be about a man. I can conceive a great mythical woman, living alone among inaccessible mountain-tops or in some lost island in the pagan seas, and ask no more. Whereas if I hear of a Hercules, I ask after Iole or Dejanira. I cannot think him a man without women. But I can think of these three deep-breasted women, living out all their days on remote hill-tops, seeing the white dawn and the purple even, and the world outspread before them for ever, and no more to them for ever than a sight of the eyes, a hearing of the ears, a far-away interest of the inflexible heart, not pausing, not pitying, but austere with a holy austerity, rigid with a calm and passionless rigidity; and I find them none the less women to the end.

And think, if one could love a woman like that once,

see her once grow pale with passion, and once wring your lips out upon hers, would it not be a small thing to die? Not that there is not a passion of a quite other sort, much less epic, far more dramatic and intimate, that comes out of the very frailty of perishable women; out of the lines of suffering that we see written about their eyes, and that we may wipe out if it were but for a moment; out of the thin hands, wrought and tempered in agony to a fineness of perception, that the indifferent or the merely happy cannot know; out of the tragedy that lies about such a love, and the pathetic incompleteness. This is another thing, and perhaps it is a higher. I look over my shoulder at the three great headless Madonnas, and they look back at me and do not move; see me, and through and over me, the foul life of the city dying to its embers already as the night draws on; and over miles and miles of silent country, set here and there with lit towns, thundered through here and there with night expresses scattering fire and smoke; and away to the ends of the earth, and the furthest star, and the blank regions of nothing; and they are not moved. My quiet, great-kneed, deep-breasted, well-draped ladies of Necessity, I give my heart to you! R. L. S.

R. L. S. attends a performance of the *Demi-Monde* by Dumas *fils*

(To William Archer)

Saranac Spring, 188–(?)

MY DEAR ARCHER,—It happened thus. I came forth from that performance in a breathing heat of indignation. (Mind, at this distance of time and with my increased knowledge, I admit there is a problem in the piece; but I saw none then, except a problem in brutality; and I still consider the problem in that case not established.) On my way down the *Français* stairs, I trod on an old gentleman's toes, whereupon with that suavity that so well becomes me, I turned about to apologise, and on the instant, repenting me of that intention, stopped the apology midway, and added something in French to this effect: No, you are one of the *lâches* who have been applauding that piece. I retract my apology. Said the old Frenchman, laying his hand on my arm, and with a smile that was truly heavenly in temperance, irony, good-nature, and knowledge of the world, "Ah, monsieur, vous êtes bien jeune!" — Yours very truly,

ROBERT LOUIS STEVENSON

Oliver Wendell Holmes returns thanks for a barometer

(To James T. Fields)

21 CHARLES STREET
July 6, 8.33 A.M.
Barometer at $30\frac{1}{10}$

MY DEAR FRIEND AND NEIGHBOUR, — Your most unexpected gift, which is not a mere token of remembrance but a permanently valuable present, is making me happier every moment I look at it. It is so pleasant to be thought of by our friends when they have so much to draw their thoughts from us; it is so pleasant, too, to find that they have cared enough about us to study our special tastes, — that you can see why your beautiful gift has a growing charm for me. Only Mrs. Holmes thinks it ought to be in the Parlor among the things for show, and I think it ought to be in the Study, where I can look at it at least once every hour every day of my life.

I have observed some extraordinary movements of the index of the barometer during the discussions which ensued, which you may be interested to see my notes of: —

Mrs. H. My dear, we shall of course keep this beautiful barometer in the parlor. *Fair.*

Dr. H. Why, no, my dear; the study is the place. *Dry.*

Mrs. H. I'm sure it ought to go in the parlor. It's too handsome for your old den. *Change.*

Dr. H. I shall keep it in the study. *Very dry.*

Mrs. H. I don't think that's fair. *Rain.*

Dr. H. I'm sorry. Can't help it. *Very dry.*

Mrs. H. It's — too — too — ba-a-ad. *Much rain.*

Dr. H. (Music omitted). 'Mid pleas-ures and paaal-a-a-c-es. *Set fair.*

Mrs. H. I *will* have it! You horrid —— *Stormy.*

You see what a wonderful instrument this is that you have given me. But my dear Mr. Fields, while it changes it will be a constant memorial of unchanging friendship: and while the dark hand of fate is traversing the whole range of mortal vicissitudes, the golden index of the kind affections shall stand always at SET FAIR.

Oliver Wendell Holmes felicitates with another young man

(To John G. Whittier)

September 2, 1889

HERE I am at your side among the octogenarians.

. . . .

You know all about it. You know why I have not thanked you before this for your beautiful and precious tribute, which would make any birthday memorable. I remember how you were overwhelmed with tributes on the occasion of your own eightieth birthday, and you can understand the impossibility I find before me of responding in any fitting shape to all the tokens of friendship which I receive. . . . I hope, dear Whittier, that you find much to enjoy in the midst of all the lesser trials which old age must bring with it. You have kind friends all around you, and the love and homage of your fellow-countrymen as few have enjoyed them, with the deep satisfaction of knowing that you have earned them, not merely by the gifts of your genius, but by a noble life, which has ripened without a flaw into a grand and serene old age. I never see my name coupled with yours, as it often is nowadays, without feeling honored by finding myself in such company, and wishing that I were more worthy of it. . . . I am living here with my daughter-in-law, and just as I turned this leaf I heard wheels at the door, and she got out, leading in in triumph her husband, His Honor, Judge Holmes of the Supreme Court of Massachusetts, just arrived from Europe by the Scythia. I look up to him as my Magistrate and he knows me as his father, but my arms are around his neck and his moustache is sweeping my cheek — I feel young again at four-score.

R. L. S. loses a friend

(To W. E. Henley)

September 19, 1883

DEAR BOY, — Our letters vigorously cross: you will ere this have received a note to Coggie: God knows what was in it.

It is strange, a little before the first word you sent me — so late — kindly late, I know and feel — I was thinking in my bed, when I knew you I had six friends — Bob I had by nature; then came the good James Walter — with all his failings — the *gentleman* of the lot, alas to sink so low, alas to do so little, but now, thank God, in his quiet rest; next I found Baxter — well do I remember telling Walter I had unearthed "a W.S. that I thought would do" — it was in the Academy Lane, and he questioned me as to the Signet's qualifications; fourth came Simpson; somewhere about the same time, I began to get intimate with Jenkin; last came Colvin. Then, one black winter afternoon, long Leslie Stephen, in his velvet jacket, met me in the *Spec.* by appointment, took me over to the infirmary, and in the crackling, blighting gaslight showed me that old head whose excellent representation I see before me in this photograph. Now when a man has six friends, to introduce a seventh is usually hopeless. Yet when you were presented, you took to them and they to you upon the nail. You must have been a fine fellow; but what a singular fortune I must have had in my six friends that you should take to all. I don't know if it is good Latin, most probably not: but this is enscrolled before my eyes for Walter: *Tandem e nubibus in apricum properat.* Rest, I suppose, I know, was all that remained; but O to look back, to remember all the mirth, all the kindness, all the humorous limitations and loved defects of that character; to think that he was young with me, sharing that weather-beaten, Fergusonian youth, looking forward through the clouds to the sun-burst; and now clean gone from my path, silent — well, well. This has been a strange awakening. Last night, when I was alone in the house, with the window open on the lovely still night, I could have sworn he was in the room with me; I could show you the spot; and, what was very curious, I heard his rich laughter, a thing I had not called to mind for I know not how long.

I see his coral waistcoat studs that he wore the first time he dined in my house; I see his attitude, leaning back a little, already with something of a portly air, and laughing internally. How I admired him! And now in the West Kirk.

I am trying to write out this haunting bodily sense of absence; besides, what else should I write of?

Yes, looking back, I think of him as one who was good, though sometimes clouded. He was the only gentle one of all my friends, save perhaps the other Walter. And he was certainly the only modest man among the lot. He never gave himself away; he kept back his secret; there was always a gentle problem behind all. Dear, dear, what a wreck; and yet how pleasant is the retrospect! God doeth all things well, though by what strange, solemn, and murderous contrivances.

It is strange: he was the only man I ever loved who did not habitually interrupt. The fact draws my own portrait. And it is one of the many reasons why I count myself honoured by his friendship. A man like you *had* to like me; you could not help yourself; but Ferrier was above me, we were not equals; his true self humoured and smiled paternally upon my failings, even as I humoured and sorrowed over his.

Well, first his mother, then himself, they are gone: "in their resting graves."

When I come to think of it, I do not know what I

said to his sister, and I fear to try again. Could you send her this? There is too much about yourself and me in it; but that, if you do not mind, is but a mark of sincerity. It would let her know how entirely in the mind of (I suppose) his oldest friend, the good, true Ferrier obliterates the memory of the other, who was only his "lunatic brother."

Judge of this for me, and do as you please; anyway, I will try to write to her again; my last was some kind of scrawl that I could not see for crying. This came upon me, remember, with terrible suddenness; I was surprised by this death; and it is fifteen or sixteen years since first I saw the handsome face in the *Spec.* I made sure, besides, to have died first. Love to you, your wife, and her sisters. — Ever yours, dear boy,

R. L. S.

I never knew any man so superior to himself as poor James Walter. The best of him only came as a vision, like Corsica from the Corniche. He never gave his measure either morally or intellectually. The curse was on him. Even his friends did not know him but by fits. I have passed hours with him when he was so wise, good, and sweet, that I never knew the like of it in any other. And for a beautiful good humour he had no match. I remember breaking in upon him once with a whole red-hot story (in my worst manner), pouring words upon him by the hour about some truck not worth an egg that had befallen me; and suddenly, some half hour after, finding that the sweet fellow had some concern of his own of infinitely greater import, that he was patiently and smilingly waiting to consult me on. It sounds nothing; but the courtesy and the unselfishness were perfect. It makes me rage to think how few knew him, and how many had the chance to sneer at their better.

Well, he was not wasted, that we know; though if anything looked liker irony than this fitting of a man out with these rich qualities and faculties to be wrecked and aborted from the very stocks, I do not know the name of it. Yet we see that he has left an influence; the memory of patient courtesy has often checked me in rudeness; has it not you?

You can form no idea of how handsome Walter was. At twenty he was splendid to see; then, too, he had the sense of power in him, and great hopes; he looked forward, ever jesting of course, but he looked to see himself where he had the right to expect. He believed in himself profoundly; but *he never disbelieved in others.* To the roughest Highland student he always had his fine, kind, open dignity of manner; and a good word behind his back.

The last time that I saw him before leaving for America — it was a sad blow to both of us. When he heard I was leaving, and that might be the last time we might meet — it almost was so — he was terribly upset, and came round at once. We sat late, in Baxter's empty house, where I was sleeping. My dear friend Walter Ferrier: O if I had only written to him more! if only one of us in these last days had been well! But I ever cherished the honour of his friendship, and now when he is gone, I know what I have lost still better. We live on, meaning to meet; but when the hope is gone, the pang comes. R. L. S.

Lieutenant-Commander Sakuma Tsutomu, of the Japanese navy, describes the sinking of his submarine. ∾ ∾ ∾ ∾ ∾ ∾

May 19, 1910

ALTHOUGH there is, indeed, no excuse to make for the sinking of his Imperial Majesty's boat and for the doing away of subordinates through my heedlessness, all on the boat have discharged their duties well, and in everything acted calmly until death. Although we are departing in pursuance of our duty to the State, the only regret we have is due to anxiety lest the men of the world may misunderstand the matter, and that thereby a blow may be given to the future development of submarines. Gentlemen, we hope you will be increasingly diligent without misunderstanding [the cause of this accident], and that you will devote your full strength to investigate everything, and so ensure the future development of submarines. If this is done, we shall have nothing to regret.

While going through gasoline submarine exercise we submerged too far, and, when we attempted to shut the sluice valve, the chain in the meantime gave way. Then we tried to close the sluice valve by hand, but it was then too late, the rear part being full of water, and the boat sank at an angle of about 25 degrees.

1. The boat rested at an incline of about 13 degrees, pointing towards the stern.

2. The switchboard being under water, the electric lights gave out. Offensive gas developed, and respiration became difficult.

At about 10 a.m. on the 15th the boat sank, and under this offensive gas we endeavoured to expel the water with a hand pump.

[1] From a translation in the "Standard."

At the same time as the vessel was being submerged, we expelled the water from the main tank. The light having gone out the gauge cannot be seen, but we know that the water has been expelled from the main tank. We cannot use the electric current entirely. The electric liquid is overflowing, but no salt water has entered, and chlorine gas has not developed. We only rely upon the hand pump now.

The above has been written under the light of the conning tower, when it was 11.45 o'clock. We are now soaked by the water that has made its way in. Our clothes are very wet and we feel cold.

I had always been used to warn my shipmates that their behaviour (on an emergency) should be calm and delicate while brave, otherwise we could not hope for development and progress, and that, at the same time, one should not cultivate excessive delicacy, lest work should be retarded. People may be tempted to ridicule this after this failure, but I am perfectly confident that my previous words have not been mistaken.

The depth gauge of the conning tower indicates 52, and, despite the endeavour to expel the water, the pump stopped and did not work after twelve o'clock.

The depth in this neighbourhood being ten fathoms, the reading may be correct.

The officers and men of submarines must be appointed from the most distinguished among the distinguished, or there will be annoyance in cases like this. Happily all the members of this crew have discharged their duties well, and I feel satisfied.

I have always expected death whenever I left my home, and therefore my will is already in the drawer at Karasaki. (This remark refers only to my private affairs, and it is not necessary. Messrs. Taguchi and Asami, please inform my father of this.)

I beg respectfully to say to his Majesty that I respectfully request that none of the families left by my subordinates shall suffer. The only matter I am anxious about now is this.

Please convey my compliments to the following gentlemen (the order may not be proper): — Minister Saito, Vice-Admiral Shimamura, Vice-Admiral Fujii, Rear-Admiral Nawa, Rear-Admiral Yamashita, Rear-Admiral Narita. (Atmospheric pressure is increasing, and I feel as if my tympanum were breaking.) Captain Oguri, Captain Ide, Commander Matsumura (Junichi), Captain Matsumura (Riu), Commander Matsumura (Kiku), my elder brother, Captain Funakoshi, Instructor Narita Kotaro, Instructor Ikuta Kokinji.

12.30 o'clock, respiration is extraordinarily difficult.

I mean I am breathing gasoline. I am intoxicated with gasoline.

Captain Nakano.[1]

It is 12.40 o'clock.

Abraham Lincoln comforts a mother

EXECUTIVE MANSION, WASHINGTON
November 21, 1864

Mrs. Bixby, Boston, Massachusetts.

DEAR MADAM, — I have been shown in the files of the War Department, a statement of the Adjutant General of Massachusetts that you are the mother of five

[1] This is the name of another officer to whom the dying officer desired to be remembered.

sons who have died gloriously on the field of battle. I feel how weak and fruitless must be any words of mine which should attempt to beguile you from your grief for a loss so overwhelming. But I cannot refrain from tendering to you the consolation that may be found in the thanks of the Republic they died to save. I pray that our heavenly Father may assuage the anguish of your bereavement and leave you only the cherished memory of the loved and lost, and the solemn pride that must be yours to have laid so costly a sacrifice upon the altar of freedom. — Yours very sincerely and respectfully

ABRAHAM LINCOLN

ACKNOWLEDGEMENTS

FOR copyright letters in the foregoing pages I am indebted to the kindness of their owners, and I am very grateful to them. A list is appended: —

Miss Janet Aldis allows me to use passages from her translations of Madame de Sévigné in *The Queen of Letter-Writers* (Methuen).

Mr. Alexander Carlyle allows me to print from the *Letters and Memorials of Jane Welsh Carlyle* (Longmans) several letters, and also three from *Early Letters of Thomas Carlyle* (Macmillan).

Messrs. Chapman & Hall allow me to make extracts from Forster's *Works and Life of Walter Savage Landor*, published by them.

Messrs. Chatto & Windus allow me to make extracts from the *Correspondence and Table Talk of B. R. Haydon.*

Mr. Buxton Forman, C.B., allows me to use the text of Keats' letters in his edition of the poet published by Messrs. Gowans & Gray.

Mr. Walter Frith allows me to print a humorous begging letter from his father's Reminiscences published by Messrs. Macmillan.

Miss Georgina Hogarth allows me to include five letters of Charles Dickens from the edition of his correspondence published by Messrs. Macmillan.

Mr. F. D. How and Messrs. Pitman allow me to use the rhyming letter of the late Bishop Walsham How, from his biography.

Mr. Roger Ingpen allows me to use his text of three letters of Shelley, as printed in his edition of the poet's correspondence published by Messrs Pitman.

Messrs. Sampson Low & Co. allow me to include two letters of O. W. Holmes from his *Life and Letters* published by them.

Messrs. Macmillan & Co. allow me to print eight letters from the correspondence of Edward FitzGerald.

Mr. Lloyd Osbourne allows me to print eight letters of R. L. S. from Messrs. Methuen's edition of his correspondence, edited by Mr. Sidney Colvin.

Mr. A. G. B. Russell allows me to use an extract from the *Letters of William Blake* (Methuen).

Miss Edith Sichel allows me to quote a letter from her memoir of Canon Ainger published by Messrs. Constable.

Other Books by E. V. LUCAS

Over Bemerton's

A Novel

After seeing modern problems vividly dissected, and after the excitement of thrilling adventure stories, it will be positively restful to drop into the cozy lodgings over Bemerton's second-hand bookstore for a drifting, delightful talk with a man of wide reading, who has travelled in unexpected places, who has an original way of looking at life, and a happy knack of expressing what is seen. There are few books which so perfectly suggest without apparent effort a charmingly natural and real personality.

Decorated cloth, $1.50

Mr. Ingleside

The author almost succeeds in making the reader believe that he is actually mingling with the people of the story and attending their picnics and parties. Some of them are Dickensian and quaint, some of them splendid types of to-day, but all of them are touched off with sympathy and skill and with that gentle humor in which Mr. Lucas shows the intimate quality, the underlying tender humanity, of his art.

Decorated cloth, 12mo, $1.35 net

Listener's Lure

A Kensington Comedy

A novel, original and pleasing, whose special charm lies in its happy phrasing of acute observations of life. For the delicacy with which his personalities reveal themselves through their own letters, "the book might be favorably compared," says the Chicago *Tribune*, "with much of Jane Austen's character work"— and the critic proceeds to justify, by quotations, what he admits is high praise indeed.

Cloth, 12mo, $1.50

PUBLISHED BY

THE MACMILLAN COMPANY

Sixty-four and Sixty-six Fifth Avenue, New York